Answering Earth's Call

TURTLE
MOON
PUBLISHING

By Gail Burkett, edited by Janis Monaco Clark, designed by Laura Wahl

New Imprint: A Game Changer Book

TurtleMoon Publishing, LLC
6656 Nez Perce Road
Bonners Ferry, ID 83805
(208) 946-9191
www.turtlemoonpublishing.com

Our Commitment to help the Earth
With dual digital publications in Kindle and PDF formats, many less paper copies
will be needed to run this book's message like mycelium from bioregion to bioregion. To offset books produced in paper form, TurtleMoon Publishing helps to fund
tree plantings through TreeSisters.org.

ISBN: 978-0-9913590-7-3
Library of Congress Control Number: 2020911997

Name: Burkett, Gail 1950 – author

Title: Answering Earth's Call

Description: Bonners Ferry, Idaho: TurtleMoon Publishing. (2020)

Identifiers: ISBN: 978-0-9913590-7-3 | Library of Congress Control Number:
2020911997

Subjects: Social aspects of: Mentoring | Drawdown Solutions | Global Warming |
Intergenerational Healing | Bioregional Education | Pachamama Communities
|Ceremony and Ritual

Dedication: To Kestrel and all children, grandchildren and great grandchildren of my friends and relations: Quite a few young relations in this new generation, newborns and those lining up to come are the Ancestors returning.

I give thanks to Olivia Lynch for her inspiration and her friends who sprinkled me with their fairy dust during the September 2019 Climate March in Sandpoint, Idaho.

Specific Gratitudes

In 2013, our book-team created TurtleMoon Publishing. I am more blessed with each passing week to have Janis Monaco Clark as editor and confidant of my life.

Fiercely loving, this is how I feel her. Without her love and honesty, this book would be unreadable. I give thanks to Janis. Dear, your editing skills and deep care are boundless.

Gifted enabler, Laura Wahl is our designer who creates an object of beauty out of mere words. She makes storytelling more fun. Blending Laura's surprising skills with Janis' helped shape this manuscript, so I'm the lucky one. From the deep well of relationship, we're blazing trails at TurtleMoon Publishing – A Place for Women's Stories. Have a look around *http://turtlemoonpublishing. com/*

Abundant Appreciations

Dearhearts,

Great Creator, God and Goddess, Earth-Gaia, Moon, Sun, and Planets, the Multiverse and Dear Kindred Spirits: As circular beings, imagine receiving love from each of these to whom we freely give love. Love is reciprocal.

Our greatest opportunity—learning to feel related to all those spinning with us in the web of the world. Related. We are all related. This lesson from the First People, draws us in and invites us to peer into the veils of our illusions. It's possible to be unified and feel grateful instead of entitled. We give thanks for all that is precious, like breathing.

This task of being human is humbling. A call and response rises from this story about teens who believe they hold the future health of all there is in their hands. They believe in stubborn optimism and opportunity: For their science project, they focused on action—the global collective can still address climate change and reverse global warming. The cascading benefits of action are infinite.

Reflecting on the forces still shaping me as an elder, memories of Women's Circles, Initiation ceremonies, and bright lights who've wanted mentoring ... I have received their deep honor and bow to the women and girls who have entered my heart through one of these front doors. All of you who have stepped inside of my hug helped create ceremonies and connecting rituals with smudge and smoke, I find your gifts irresistible. Our long weaving—filled with song, drumming and dance, most of all with long conversations—coalesces into this story and comes as a gift back to you.

I felt compelled by questions: Why did the Dalai Lama say, "The world will be saved by western woman?" Who are these women? Why is the Sector for Women and Girls the #1 solution to reversing global warming according to *Drawdown.org*? And the most haunting question, what will I say when my grandchildren ask how did I respond to the threat of climate change?

After the Climate March in September, Equinox weekend 2019 I entered an altered state, an annoyed state. I wanted a community to share about the possibilities of community, of regenerating a bioregion, ultimately to reverse global warming. I didn't feel very related and I couldn't see the possibility of holding a community together.

For 100 days, I gave myself over to writing from the dark into the dawn to the tricky melodies of many Mockingbirds. There was one in every tree at West

Wetlands in Yuma along the Colorado River. This work I called *A Story*; each day it summoned the image of a fire circle where Ancestors created myths to guide the people. Inspiration also came from *A Wrinkle in Time*: I freely shape-shifted from my winter-camp to the small villages where my people need elder help—like igniting curiosity, giving permission, revealing opportunities, harvesting from life's experience, and connecting generations. I was free to express my vivid, repressed imagination. I invite you to read and allow your imaginations to wander. Vivid and free.

Through the research—which uncovered truly bleak news about our Earth and her changing climates—all you kindred spirits offered comfort to me. How I would like to save you from scientific truths about the tipping points! Storytelling has a greater capacity than any other force on this planet. For many years I have felt frozen by the bleakness of the reality behind infinite layers of illusions. Even when revealed otherwise, things appear to be fine. Maybe you also share this frozen state, but let's explore the collective action of villagers, awake, hip, concerned. Action can cure all psychological states of un-ease.

In the same way that teens sprinkle old women with fairy dust to keep the energy moving, old women pour wisdom into the vessels of teens. Mutuality develops over time and silently spreads village values of generosity, kindness, and hilarity.

Opening to heart-way, join me in giving thanks to the very real Circle of Consultants whose cameo appearances in this work of fiction helped me see a new level of support for teens. Let's give thanks to the four Scholars, completely fictitious 17-year olds who reflect many girls I have known. Unlike these imaginary teens, the women in this book are related to me, they are the beating heart of home in Idaho. When you see the word Consultant, interpret it as elegant elders who know their strengths. Let's also give thanks to their significant others.

At that Climate March, two little seeds quickened: Fairy dust sprinkled by teen girls met with my desire for a Pachamama Alliance Community. Voila! A winter's writing retreat created this story as a gift, mine to give and yours to receive. In this exchange—the formula for love—you and I become more related.

Boundaries have blurred between me and all these adorable women and girls who practice relationship. We have direct experience that it takes a village to raise our children. Let's practice our skills together.

Namaste and great love, Gail Burkett
Bonners Ferry, Idaho July 2020

Contents

Consider water for a moment.

Upright and filled with snowmelt, surely a seer will appreciate this ancient water hole made by spring runoffs. Holy water. Life. Thirst quencher. Purifier, friend in the astral world where spirits abound.

Watch yourself and your progeny spin through the world.

Generational adoration, this is a thread. Mentee and mentor both are teachers.

If you are inclined to listen to silence to be cleansed of the stress and strain of modern living, you might love water gazing. Pick a stone that has a lot to say, a door will open in your Earth-heart.

Remember what the Dali Llama said, "Western woman will save the Earth." It must be so. Gather your circle around you. Earth is asking for this from her women - how can you be present?

How can you serve?

You will wonder where the ideas come from. Directly from relations with Earth and her elements, this is the answer from water, directly from God and Goddess, of course.

Chapter 1

ON LIMBS OF ALL BEINGS

On that sparkly afternoon of Christmas Day, they rode the quad chair together up Schweitzer Mountain. Unable to hold back, Jules said, "Hey, let's be a team on the Project." Left hands popped out of gloves to pinky-swear across their laps. It was agreed and nothing more needed to be said.

Jules connected her past to her future—was it Gran who taught her that trick to bridge time? Shh-this is holiday time. What is time anyway? Fall quarter had been intense and Jules remembered sweating bullets over a couple of grades. In less than two weeks school would start up again. STEM-Advanced: the legendary Project of Second Half creeped into her holiday fun.

The next moments on the chairlift became frozen in time. Only twice before, Alex thought. Sara let out a squeaky peep, "Not ever." The ermine stood still, as if to connect with the four girls. They all saw this little anomaly at the same time. Their favorite thing in all the world. Back when they were little girls, days at camp under the stars in their sleeping bags, they fell to sleep telling such wildlife stories.

White on white, rather small, feet and tail moved like a cloud over the Sun. With all the feeling of illusion, the little colorless weasel darted over the snow and disappeared in a straight line into the woods. Each girl clutched her heart and swooned. That sighting was incredibly precious. This animal ally had blessed their decision to do a Project together. Were those tears of gratitude behind their goggles?

All white against the snow except its tail tipped in black, the tiny critter caused Jules to hold her breath. Finally, Dot said, "Rare." She realized two things—she was holding her breath and her newly formed team had seen it too. Wildlife sightings were continuous fun. For a decade of knowing one another, they had collected and shared stories even though their only incentive was love. "Remember *A Wrinkle in Time*? Our ermine is like that."

There had been new snow on Christmas Eve. Now, as the speedy new chairlift pulled and their bodies felt the steep angle at the top, Jules turned around to see Lake Pend Oreille ten miles away. Their lake. They played as kids at City Beach. This is the icon of the north. Unloaded from the chair with her friends, she swooned again. This year she was decked out in four colors of purple. Jules couldn't decide if it all looked stunning or ghastly. Her hat slightly bright and blingy was a different purple than her scarf or her jacket. At Goodwill last year, as the ski season ended, winter gear was practically a give-away.

Five seconds of thought to her appearance was all she ever needed to be bored. Remembering that Sara required some help off the top, eye contact was more important. Before she dropped her goggles over her face, "Follow my line, I'll go slow right here at the top." Beyond the Black Diamond, Sara was a fine skier. These four young women were friends because of little kindnesses.

More an instigator than leader, Jules said, "See if you can feel the Mountain Spirit. Can you become One with that Spirit? Let's practice."

After lobbing the question and seeing her friends nod in agreement as they adjusted their goggles and tightened their boot buckles, Jules had the best ski-run of her life. Last year she had read Dolores LaChapelle's gorgeous little book about the ecstatic feeling of skiing powder snow. In her daydreams, Jules imagined being with Dolores on one of those deep powder days. The book and its famous quotes were texted back and forth all last year. This group had been so happy to find a woman mountaineering guide like Dolores. She was great-grandmother age, and inside their budding inner minds, invincible. Dolores skied from the 50s through the 70s at Alta, Utah. After that, she wrote the most radical books about the Earth and a philosophy of care and mutuality with all living things.

Once, Alex sent around a text from Dolores, *"Skiing powder shows us how to live." Dolores LaChapelle.* Included in the text were her own weather observations: *"Except snow is becoming a climate issue."* Through the winter of 2019, they didn't have good snow until late in the season.

In the warming hut, the girls had added hot cider to their water bottles. It costs less to share and it's mighty good. The naturalist in the group is Dot, but sometimes she surprises with her research. "It's true, we can read the data. We have fewer powder days and our snow – overall – has less water content."

Alex laughed. "Since my legs have grown so long," she kicked her ski-boot into the air, "we have had less powder. It didn't measure 8 inches today."

Sara lifted her water bottle to reverse the negative, "I had the run of my life!"

Jules said, "Me too. Do you think that was ecstasy?"

Dot started a journal entry in the air with her index finger. "Here's the headline for my journal: Teammates sighted an ermine on Christmas Day and took their blessing for Advanced Placement Project 2020." They beamed at each other and jumped on the SPOT Bus.

At home that afternoon the sun dropped behind Baldy Mountain early. The family packed up Christmas and dishes for dinner and went to Gran's log cabin in the woods. Jules pulled the little book of Dolores' off her shelf and stuffed it into her backpack. After she read *Deep Powder* from the library last year, she gave it as a gift to her dad, Jordi. The subject of philosophy entered their house through an iconic woman and began to expand.

Dolores had guided Jules life as a book mentor for the past year and Jules freely shared this philosophy with her friends. She sent around quotes as texts and they wrote back about how it made them feel. Then Alex's text arrived and snow as a climate issue rattled Jules for weeks and months. The literal chaos in weather didn't offer a deep core layer of snow to ski on until February. She could trace the beginning of her love for the Earth back to a single root, but her mind offered new gifts this past year. Connections, consequences, relationships between things, these were science concepts whole careers were built upon, her father had told her.

Jules' Mom, Robin, took the subject of development most seriously. The day when Jules handed her a text thread to read, everything changed between mother and daughter. One smart kid was pushing the envelope every day and Robin decided this was miraculous. The text had started as a pasted quote. Jules and Alex had a legendary ski day, run after run, first tracks side by side. Dolores has written this same thing happened with her friend.

> Joy is the response of a lover receiving what he loves. This is the joy we feel when skiing powder. This overflowing gratitude is what produces the absolutely stupid, silly grins that we always flash at one another at the bottom of a powder run. We all agree that we never see these grins anywhere else in life.
>
> -Dolores LaChapelle

Jules had been so pixie-like until middle school. Curious about everything, she flitted from subject to subject like a butterfly visits flowers—briefly. Jordi and Robin had considered this fleeting curiosity as a stage. It became a family joke, especially since Samantha was so keen and focused. Just a year apart, the sisters couldn't be more different. They were both blondies from Robin's genes, but that was about it for sister similarities. Their eyes and noses also looked similar and this was how people guessed they were sisters.

One day Jules and Alex compared notes. What was their interest in science? It seemed like they took the same science electives. This was new information, tracking personal patterns of the scholastic subjects that shaped their thinking. All the girls shared book lists. Jules and Alex were just about the only ones reading non-fiction. Biographies or autobiographies of women scientists were their personal favorites. Rachel Carson topped each of their lists.

Jules knew her hard work in science was shaped like a funnel. Since age ten in the 4th grade when Robin helped her discover that her way of learning was mostly visual, Jules began making drawings to explain things to herself. Ms. Perky Hagadon's 6th grade science class ignited something. The 9th grade trip to Costa Rica prepped Jules for AP-Biology and then AP-Environmental Science in 10th grade.

Each run when she flew down the mountain, Jules felt part of it, at one, as Gran would say. Especially after reading *Their Day in the Sun* about the women of the Manhattan Project, Jules felt excited to do something science-y and fun with her teammates. Searching for her patterns, she knew her heart connected to something. She started to visualize the funnel leading to Climate Science. The next afternoon a miracle happened.

Gran needed help cleaning the cabins, so Jules stayed behind when the family drove back to Sandpoint. It had always been more fun to visit the dude ranch and ride each of the horses one by one. She had been on three different Western Pleasure horses since break began, and today she had her pick again.

"Jules, will you take this book to lost and found?" Gran asked. Without even looking at it, she hugged it to her chest with both arms. On the run, she took a shortcut over to the main building. Slipping on the snow was half the fun, staying on her feet barely, then the tree root took her down. Before the snow, it was easier to see that big old root seeking a permanent connection to air and water. In one creepy second, the bone made an audible crack and her movement stopped.

Laying on the gurney the day after Christmas, after the pinky swear that formed their Project team, Jules still clutched the book of the errand. Relaxing with an aspirin tonic, she opened the front cover: *Drawdown. The only plan.* She swore later she could see light bulbs going off. This would do nicely for their big Project, and with a broken leg, she could lead the charge. Something struck her as funny.

When her Gran reached for the book, Jules felt possessive but had a gleam in her eye. "Oh Gran, I'm going to do some good, just like you always say." They were both still in their riding jeans, although Jules' jeans had been sliced up to her thigh because the bone poked through her skin. Her long braid had not been renewed that day, but she didn't care. For horse riding it was always coiled under her old felt fedora.

Instead of the book, Gran asked, "You must have your phone in there somewhere." Deep in her Carhartt jacket, it sounded the vibrate buzz. Digging it out, Jules put in her passcode and glanced: sixteen text messages. Handing it to Gran, Jules sighed. Gran took it and said, "Shall we document this event?" Jules gave her automatic camera-smile, but it wasn't sincere.

Gran had just snapped a couple of photos of Jules when the doctor appeared. A nurse had given her a shot of morphine and another for nausea. "We're going right into the helicopter and over to Spokane for surgery. Are you comfortable enough?" he asked Jules.

Robin, who had rounded the corner and tiptoed to the head of the gurney to kiss and smooth Jules' hair, told Gran she was going with Jules. "Yes. Great. After I finish chores, I'll drive over with Jordi," Gran reasoned. Both women knew the drill. There was very little thrill in a flight for life. The time just ahead included a long surgery for Jules and longer waits around sterile comfort rooms.

"Here's your phone. I got a couple of shots of you holding *Drawdown*." Gran gave Jules her twinkling eye, "Your claim to fame is in there somewhere." Gran became the first to learn of the secret of the book and the Project. "It will turn out alright, you'll see. I'll bring clean jeans and your charger from the ranch. Text me anything else. Love ya, Jules."

Blowing kisses as she always did, "Love ya more, Gran."

Jules' Junior Science Class studied the Manhattan Project in the first quarter. They read two books about the women behind the scenes who had become brilliant physicists, chemists, mathematicians, biologists, and technicians in the labs. Jules especially liked the secret project in Oak Ridge Tennessee, which told the story in more intimate detail. After reading *The Girls of Atomic City*, her favorite of the two books, Jules began to dream about doing good. Like Gran said, "Always deliver it with an eye twinkle." Jules spent hours in front of the mirror trying to perfect the twinkle eye that her grandmother used, dazzling when it came your way.

Robin, holding her hand in the helicopter, leaned in close. She worked at the hospital in Sandpoint, she'd been briefed by the doctor's first assistant. She leaned in further to speak over the noise of the blades. "It's a bad one, Jules. Your tibia kind of exploded. Let's see what the Spokane team can do. Will you be brave?"

Through new tears, Jules asked her Mom, "We will be brave together right? Dad's been through worse."

Jules dabbed the tears with her sleeve and felt the roughness of her jacket, "Owee, that didn't feel good." She closed her eyes. This was how she had prayed for her dad when he was in a similar situation; he survived gangrene in his leg. Prayer was easy. She had been a "None" since middle school. Her treatise to herself took a whole year to develop, but when she finished her final 8th grade English paper, she was clear about her beliefs.

There was no reason to follow Gran into Buddhism or her Napa, California grandparents either. They were Catholics but not very devout. She felt really good about prayer, just not the organized part. Her mom and dad had given her the choice to be her own decider and this worked for her. She squeezed her eyes tighter against her discomfort and the helicopter's noise and prayed for herself. It was easy to find her voice to God inside her heart without a church or its dogma. Yes, her connection was strong. A little morphine helped her enter the cloud. She thought about her Root.

Chapter 2

EMERGENCY MEDICINE ROCKS

Greeting the chopper, a short man in scrubs reassured her. "We're going to do our best to put your leg back together, Julia." He continued talking to her, keeping eye contact while the team prepped her for surgery. "Have you heard of artificial bone? With a plate and screws providing a foundation from the far side, your body will grow new bone."

"Please call me Jules, Doctor ... "

"You can call me Doctor Jim."

She thought he was cute, grey hair and all, and she was going to trust him. Maybe it was his eye twinkle, or maybe his short stature, but she felt fine after a half hour of strong praying.

Announcing her bravery at the cast-signing party three days after her fall from Heaven to Earth, Jules held up her X-ray. Newly off pain pills, she said, "I am only going to say this one time, then you'll see my brave face. My tibia was wrenched sideways through the skin. Ligaments were torn above and below, so this knee and ankle were involved but not broken." She pointed and waited for the sighs of drama to stop.

"Doctor Jim designed a new bone with cleaned-up fragments, glued them together with artificial bone and a little cadaver bone, attached ligaments, and stitched. Say a little prayer for all that's going on under this cast." The surgery had taken four hours. She really didn't feel brave yet; she felt sick in her heart.

First in line for drama, Sara placed her hand over Jules' and said, "Brave? I'm in shock, aren't you? I mean, we were skiing while you were in surgery because you didn't answer our texts."

Alex had her head down, drawing all over the cast. "Ya, fuck, Jules. Thank goodness it's only your leg," She cussed like a logger, she'd been told. One hand held her long blond mane out of her eyes.

Robin was not far away. The girls' colorful language only elicited an open eye blink. That battle was not one to fight. She added a couple of details. "Her surgery was extra-long, so Jules is confined to bed for a week. The trick to healing this mess will be in the blood flow. We will be doing therapy five times a day to encourage the capillaries to regrow." She unpacked a large box filled with gadgets. The therapy apparatus took up half the floor space at the end of Jules' bed. Jordi remembered his own ordeal and was going to make logistics easier for Jules. Her bed now occupied the living room, opposite the front door.

"We will invest in therapy and gadgets instead of a used car for Jules."

Bravely, Jules said, "I don't need a car now. Seriously, in six weeks I'll be free-walking and in eight weeks the final cast comes off. Sign here for immortality; I will make you famous. This lasts only three weeks. What if that was all the time we had to live?"

Dot had not said a word beyond hello. "I need to get past my shock," she said and doubled up her fist, pretending to punch Jules in the arm. "I'm not dying until our Project is over."

Jules squealed, "Oh! Let me tell you what I've been reading over there in Spokane." Her friends leaned in, expecting it to be juicy.

She reached under her blanket for the book. "Do you remember the three climate marches this year? Do you remember how we've been agonizing what to do besides giving out our emails to join other protesters? I found the answer. Actually, it's why I broke my leg. If you look for the silver lining, good things happen right along with the bad things."

Jules had remembered this while she was still in the helicopter. Now she tried hard to give each of her BFF teammates a sparkling eye, turning the book around so they could read the title. "I get goose bumps every time I read the whole title—*Drawdown: The Most Comprehensive Plan Ever Proposed to Reverse Global Warming.*" She waved the book in the air and showed off the marks on many pages while her mom began their therapy routine.

Jules explained that the scholars who wrote this book combined math and storytelling. "Here's the longer version of my story: This book was left in one of the guest cabins, conspicuously, like we were supposed to find it. My errand was to deliver this book to our lost and found box. I never let go of it, not even when I hit the ground. I clutched it right up until surgery and made them give it back to me after.

"When Dad saw the book on the chair in the hospital, he remembered hearing through the grapevine—you know, he has secret sources—that Gail Burkett had tried to organize a community. The whole family knew Gail from the Northside Garden Club, but here was new insight into this quiet elder. She wanted only to talk about the climate crisis and this book. He immediately called her. She was shocked to hear from him. His source was correct, she had been at the Climate March in September. Do any of you remember giving our emails to her? Even the mayor gave away his email, so we see the grapevine at work like the weave of a spider."

Sara pulled a face and under her breath, "Fuck no. I missed the march 'cause we went to Banff for Mom's birthday. I'm still mad about that, but those Canadian Rockies are powerfully beautiful. Dex is determined to share his favorite places with me and Jon."

Looking to Alex and Dot, "We all gave Gail our school emails, remember?" Dot whined a little, "Who looks at those?"

"I didn't even look at my emails last quarter," Alex said. "You know, volleyball consumed me."

Sara reached for the book and Jules surrendered it. "Impressive! Look at all your tabs and sticky notes."

On the phone, Gail had explained to Jordi about her email campaign, her fingers had been crossed, hoping to spark a community. She was trying to create an opening to the schools. Jordi agreed, as the middle school math teacher, he knows all about the curriculum struggles that teachers have. He's an easy-going guy and told Gail his curiosity was awake to Solutions.

"I read the whole book in two days," Jules bragged. "This book is the real deal. The stories read like the magic we felt when we saw our ermine. Scientists went looking for wisdom and found hands-on practices from people who care about the Earth and its places. *Drawdown* is filled with stories we can share in our own community. Dad says the math is impressive.

"When Gail came to visit me this morning, she had her book in her bag. It's all marked up with color tabs and she gave me some tabs. I marked some of the same pages she had marked. If you all agree, she will ghost our Project. She has a PhD in women's studies, but Dad said, she's low key about herself. Before she left she asked me, "Have you read Madeleine L'Engle's book, *A Wrinkle in Time*? It's the story of a teen girl who is transported on an adventure through space and time."

Not only was that their favorite book, they had each performed a role in their 9th grade play. Jules was the heroine, Meg Murry. Jules' mom had become a devotee of Madeleine L'Engle, too. When they first met as the behind-the-scenes support network for their girls, the parents agreed that for teen women, outside experiences and books the family shared, count as much as school, probably more in these challenging times. That's the one thing parents can control.

Sara straightened the bedspread, parked her rump and one knee half-way on the bed and opened the book flat to a large sticky note. She squealed, "OMG! WHF? Look at this dude riding a reindeer. Seriously? Why do you have a big sticky on this page? It says, 'coming attractions.'"

Alex handed the markers to Sara and reached for the book. She had just drawn skulls all over the cast, "This is our Project? I was thinking something local like the oil trains, the smelter, or water quality. This is much sexier. I want to ride a reindeer."

"Isn't that a bit far-fetched," Dot said, reading over Alex's shoulder. "Repopulating the Earth's largest biome called the mammoth steppe?" The image was dreamy, a herd of reindeer moving through the mist with a guy in the middle mounted on one of the reindeer. "It's stunning to look at, though."

Alex was animated. "I remember all three climate marches. It says here," pointing to the front cover, "this is a plan to reverse global warming. Is this what Gail was talking about when we gave her our emails?"

Jules groaned during her mom's manipulations; there was an instrument cupped over her hand and she was massaging Jules' upper thigh. Jules raised both hands because she was dying to speak.

"I've had time to look at those eight or nine emails Gail sent; she sounded so hopeful in each one. She plans to go wide to the community in the spring and wants our help. We've had the climate education thanks to Mr. Hastings. Ouch!"

"Sorry, I'm trying to be invisible here," her mother said.

Alex danced around Jules' living room with the book across her heart. "I didn't know Gail from Northside like you did because I was homeschooled through elementary. Remember? You mentioned her name in Perky's class. I know that because I was jealous I didn't learn gardening. From middle school, we all shared the same science classes. I was the biggest nerd in that class because I knew more than any of you—so I thought."

From way up the main watershed, the Upper Pack, homeschooling had been an obvious solution to education. When Alex's parents Deborah and Joe, Jr. divorced a couple of years ago, Deborah moved to Lakeside Drive in Sagle. This gave Alex the lake but pulled her away from her grandparents and her dad.

"Ya, not! I'm a lot more gifted than you." Dot remembered how smart Alex was when she arrived in the 7th grade science class. "I fought you for highest score on every test, you're a tough competitor. We both lived too far away then."

Reaching into one pocket of her tight jeans, she said, "Now I'm the only one who lives in the wilderness, but you can count on me." She dangled three keys. "My dad gave up his Mustang for Christmas, so I am officially contributing to emissions. He thought I needed to practice generosity; he claims that's why."

With a little sashay around the bed, she repeated, "Mine as long as I practice kindness and generosity."

Alex was quick as lightning and grabbed the keys, startling Dot. Suddenly everyone was talking at once, "A car! We have a car!"

"Correction. I have a car to get back and forth from the Creek and," Dot flashed her dimples and all her teeth, "to serve up kindness. When I told my dad that was hokey, he made up a song called *Hokey*. You know him, he feels guilty, so he showers us with gifts. He said I can trade it in on an electric car if I work to subsidize solar panels for electric charging."

Dot's dad was a helicopter pilot. Even though they gardened and hunted to live off the land, their abundance from those woods came at a cost. He was gone at least half the time because of his special skills. "Last week we talked about the car while we rode up the chairlift. Dad's a great skier and hard to keep up with, but I managed. He thinks I am obscene because I don't want to put gasoline into his precious car."

Using her eyes expressively, Dot reported what she said to her dad. "He called me a *paradigm shifter* because I said, 'Dad, using more emissions is outside of my belief system now.' Turns out he has an inner argument with himself because his whole world is built with emissions. He drives to the airport, flies to his job, loads up his helicopter with flight-fuel and flies all day. You know, just to come home, he doubles his emissions. We wouldn't exist without gasoline!"

Dot truly felt torn about living in the wilderness and needing to come to school. *#FridaysforFuture* made it easy for Dot to stay home on Fridays and post endlessly about teens protesting all around the globe. "Dad told me about an incredible book he was reading, *The Overstory*, by Richard Powers that began to loosen his thinking and he wondered how we could use the literary novel to begin a conversion, a U-turn from our colossal wrong turn."

Because the book was about radical activism and saving trees, they all agreed to share the audio version of *The Overstory* from Dot.

Chapter 3

FIRST LIBRARY MEETING

The New Year came in with a deep blanket of snow. The placement of the holidays on the calendar gave everyone a long vacation. On January 7, school started up again. Relieved to be mobile after a week in bed, Jules' grandma delivered her to Sandpoint High in a snazzy new wheelchair rental. "What a way to start your New Year, Jules. You will likely remember this time over Christmas and New Year's as a Rites of Passage. When everyone wants to make a fuss over you, let them. This is your return to community."

Since their STEM class met on odd days, Alex wheeled Jules to the library that first day back while Dot drove Sara to pick up cookies before joining them. The community library was quiet after lunch compared to after school.

Gathering her team back around a circular foyer table, Jules suggested, "Let's start wherever you want. I was thinking of booking a study room to show the two-hour movie that goes with this book. Gail showed me how to sign on. The video is called *Introduction to Drawdown* and it has tons of supplemental material. An organization, the Pachamama Alliance, in the San Francisco Bay Area also put together a five-part Getting-into-Action Workshop to go beyond the Introduction. If you look in the front, this book was published in 2017, almost three years ago."

After this speech, Alex pulled her hair up in a high ponytail and protested. "I did spend time on the Drawdown website. It's a maze with lots of bells and whistles, and data." She emphasized what she liked best. "But I didn't see anything called *Introduction to Drawdown* or anything called Pachamama."

"I really like that word, Pachamama, it feels familiar to me. Isn't that a past-life thing, when something foreign feels familiar?" Sara was always dramatic, and her questions were as far-out as possible. Her long, dark afro looked just like her favorite role models.

Jules jumped in again because she was bursting with information. "I've had a couple of Zooms with Gail and she told me the book was featured in a course offered by the Pachamama Alliance which advocates for Indigenous Peoples' rights and Rights of Nature. Gail learned about Drawdown from them. The movie came out later, this past year in fact. She shared her screen and showed me how she signs onto the forum pages, pretty cool social media." Trying to lift herself off the wheelchair seat, Jules' dimple exaggerated her frown.

"Each one of us needs our own password when we apply with our personal email." There was that thing again, email. "When I admitted to Gail that we had not even seen her emails, she was surprised.

"Okay, I want to share just this little bit more. All around the world, hub communities are studying the book and have begun doing projects. I suspect we may not be the only ones doing a Drawdown entry for Class Project, but we will be the best."

Jules pulled loose pages from her book and fanned them in front of her face as if she was over-heated. "Phew, I'm just getting started. There are lots of multi-color pie charts to inspire us, so I did one for the Panhandle." Everyone huddled around. "Since there are only five of us, counting Gail, we can put her to work because she volunteered. We each need a major category and at least one Solution for our orals."

Giving each of her teammates the sparkling eye, "We need a plan, who's best at that?"

Sara passed around the cookies they bought at the co-op, complaining, "I had a sugar letdown. You know, first day back." She took a big bite and said with her mouth full, "These are allowed because they are gluten free."

Jules talked over the top of her friends as they reached for cookies. "Gail said we begin with the end in mind, just like an architect. When I told her how smart that sounded, she credited her husband, Kenny. He taught her that so she could finish her PhD."

Waving her pie chart around, Jules continued. "These broad categories are only suggested ways of seeing the totality of what we have here in our Kootenai Bioregion. Notice, the circle is divided five ways."

Everyone leaned in, amazed at all the work Jules had done. "Pizzazz," Dot said. "It's her secret weapon."

Jules beamed. "While you were all skiing, Gail came to the house twice, like through the wrinkle in time. This pie covers the place we call home, everything we have in the *chimney*, what Gail calls our two northern counties in the Idaho Panhandle." She demonstrated: thumb and index on each hand touching to form a rectangular in the air. Jules handed each of her friends a sheet of paper. "Flip it for our assignments. Of course, you get to choose."

On one of their Zooms, Gail had said Jules was brilliant. Actually, she was simply hard-working and needed to keep focused so she didn't feel sorry for herself. Her sister, Samantha, and her parents had skied two days after New Year's, but they brought home Thai food take-out, her fave. Jules was happy to be busy. Her dad even hooked up the printer on the headboard through Blue-tooth, so she didn't have to get off the bed.

On the back of her first pie chart, Jules had prepared the broad definitions: Bonner and Boundary County, Idaho: 3,192 miles; population, 56,675; notable qualities—6 rivers, 20 creeks, and 100 lakes. The front showed five color Sec-tors to study the Drawdown approach to reversing global warming. Dot stood up and read them out loud. As she read, creating a little echo in the foyer, she began to recognize the perimeters of their Project.

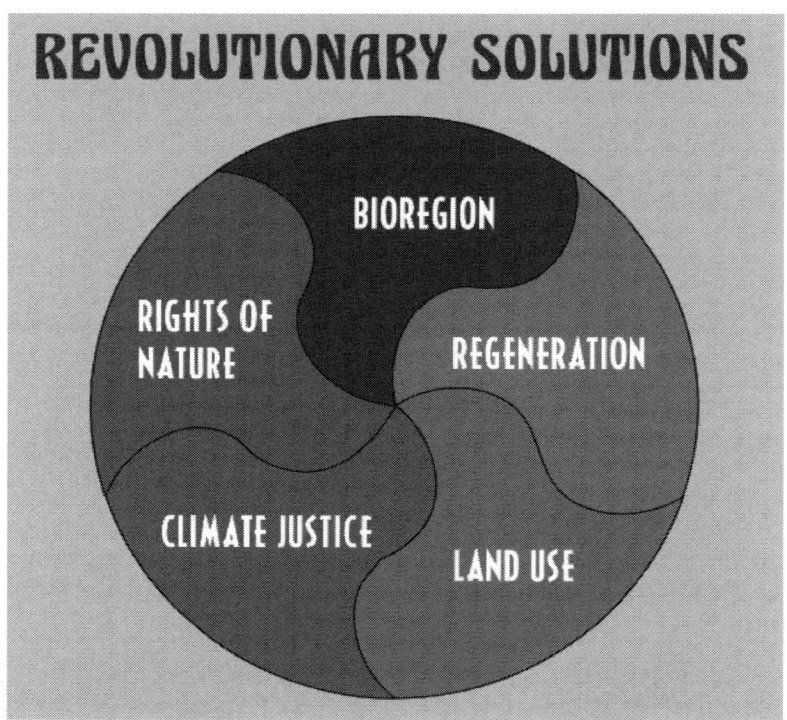

REVOLUTIONARY SOLUTIONS

BIOREGION
RIGHTS OF NATURE
REGENERATION
CLIMATE JUSTICE
LAND USE

- **BIOREGION**—includes every person plus a thorough geographic, cultural, and ecosystem inventory.
- **REGENERATION**—a strategy and a Solution; it can blanket our rural area with a science answer to the climate crises: Farmers and gardeners unite to increase photosynthesis.

- **CLIMATE JUSTICE**—affects everyone who lives here, also migrations of people and critters. We need a plan for hundreds, maybe thousands of migrating strangers. No CO_2 number is attached to Justice; this is where our humanity meets our values.
- **SPIRIT OF CHANGE**—picks up a thread from the old climate action network, Citizen's Climate Action Network (CCAN), to move beyond the carbon footprint into nourishment for our bodies and beliefs about climate with the interfaith community.
- **RIGHTS OF NATURE**—Local laws need to be passed to protect mountains, rivers, lakes, and forests.

Dot sat quietly through her second cookie. "Right. Organization—designing like architects by seeing six months ahead. That will be our direction, our North Star. Awesome work, Jules."

Alex watched Jules get a neck rub from Robin who was setting up Jules' therapy. Reaching up under her messy ponytail, she rubbed her own neck.

"This is edgy stuff, but your pie chart makes it all clear. Let's go with it for this week, at least, and see how we feel on Friday.

"Add my name. I choose BIOREGION because I've been to all the boundaries and I think I see the whole picture. I will need help with inventory. What do we count?"

Moving with mystery, Gail emerged from the direction of the bathroom and asked a question. "Can you riff on trees, each one of your wildlife sightings, kids, native plants, gardeners, farmers, anyone who grows living things, nurseries? Ready, set, go!" Beaming, Gail pointed her finger toward the ceiling. "Alex, naming is your job in this bioregion topic. First, start with what you know and what your friends know. Ask your parents to riff with you. This Project is a cooperative and collaborative affair. We want to upscale every good thing about our place on Earth." Gail circled the table, touched each girl, and gave Robin a little hug.

Groaning with pleasure as Robin rubbed her neck and down her back, Jules jumped in. "Fruit trees! Sprouts will help, he's our gleaner and local fruit tree expert, right?" After finishing two therapy sessions for her knee and thigh, she accepted help getting back into her wheelchair. Then her mom disappeared, lugging the big box with her. "There's a guy named Kaz in Bonners Ferry," Jules continued. "And Georgia the cherry lady knows things."

Gail spoke up. "We need to count acres of forests, number of cows—you can choose the list. This may be like an Achilles' heel for you Alex, because your grandfather and father are loggers. My grandad and great uncle were Idaho loggers too, from another generation."

Noticing Alex's grimace, Jules quickly added, "Knowing that gives you a great advantage. Maybe we could help imagine how to retrain all of our loggers to leave the remaining trees for at least a decade."

The girls had texted this idea over the past summer because they had seen so many logging trucks along Highway 95. Alex exhaled deeply. She looked at Gail. "I took the Ecology class last year; I've known for a long time that you're right. Over the 4th of July, Dad tried to take all of us kids fishing on the St. Joe because it's his namesake river. When we saw the clear-cut mountains, two of them, we pulled over. Dad and Grandad just sat and stared.

"My memory of those two mountains will flash as eyesores for the rest of my life. I can't imagine ever going up that river again. Dad and Gramps were truly shaken and didn't stop talking about how it ruined their blue-ribbon fishing forever. I sat in the back seat and shrunk down, thinking how long forever might be."

Jules wrote, ALEX, beside BIOREGION and turned to Dot. "You know me and key words," Dot said. "When you sent around a picture of Drawdown, I went searching for Paul Hawken. You will not believe what I found." They all leaned in. "YouTube videos! Lots of beautiful messages from Paul have been clipped and posted. This guy sounds so soft and humble, but he's like a rock star." She could tell she had overdone her praise.

"I understood the magnitude of this book by watching Paul speak about Project Drawdown. I'll send you two videos you should see right away." Everyone's phone vibrated at the same time. I choose REGENERATION because Paul does; that's the name of his next book." She was shining like when love shows up. Jules wrote, DOT, beside REGENERATION.

Gail spoke up. "I have to confess; research is all I've done for the last three years away from my farm and I am 100% committed for the next ten years." She planned on going to the Panhandle Alliance for Education—PAFE—for support later that day. "Next meeting, I am showing you the movie *Introduction to Drawdown*. Personally, after imagining 80 SOLUTIONS from my vantage point in Boundary County, I can't wait for you to see it. After you watch the movie a couple of times, we could take it to the middle school science classes and teach other kids. You know, practice presenting. For your own classmates, you might want to know there is also an Action Workshop. You will discover the fun of presenting."

When they took a bathroom break, Gail excused herself to meet with someone at PAFE, before the office closed.

No one saw her come out of the bathroom. "Gail is here and gone so quickly," Alex noticed. "I've never seen anyone quite like her before." She delivered a twinkle eye to Jules and said, "As long as you're laid up, would you keep working to make this into our introductory chart on PowerPoint?"

Jules exhaled. "I'm working on memes for us too. After I told Gail about our extra credential in science, I had to show her pictures. The photos from Costa Rica help when I feel sorry for myself," she looked at Dot. "Remember?" Two of the girls had joined their science teacher in Costa Rica for Christmas break the year before. Dot and Jules looked at each other and exclaimed simultaneously. "Costa Rica!"

Alex punched the air with both fists, "It sucks that we didn't go together."

Dot added, "Such a drama queen. Perky would be so proud of us now, having our first brainstorm."

When she cleared her throat and wiggled her fingers in the air, signaling she had something to say, everyone turned to Sara. "I've always been envious of your trips with Perky. You all know I would choose the hardest from this list. I've been talking to my dad about a recent NY Times story that shows how sea level will rise massively, permanently flooding coastal cities and swelling coastal rivers. Think about Portland on the Columbia. What happens to the city when the river rises with the sea?

"This is going to happen. We can't stop it now. Our future has been altered. I want to go to Portland next year for my gap year." She started to cry, and everyone fell silent.

"Yup, that's my motivating example, I think. Portlanders will be moving to Sandpoint. Write me down for CLIMATE JUSTICE; it's good to be a lawyer's daughter. I want to include the disadvantaged people here first. Before I even saw our list and before I had a name for it, I asked Jon to go around with me to interview the cooking crews at our soup kitchens in Sandpoint. Dex, my other dad, cooks at the Hoot Owl, eight days a week, he says. Justice and fair-share will be my ruse, is that the right word?"

Jules wanted to stand up and everyone wanted to help her. Instead she released her arms and sunk deeper into her wheelchair with a grunt and said, "Fair-trade? A good journalist doesn't need a trick to ask questions. Fair-share and fair-trade are both good idioms, Sara. We may need to slice the pie for that, it seems like a stretch, but economics is part of justice, isn't it?"

Holding up her phone, Sara was seriously scribbling with her thumbs, notes to self about this juicy conversation. Jules had written Fair-share along the margin where Climate Justice held one-fifth of their Team chart. Jules wrote, SARA, next to CLIMATE JUSTICE.

"Me? I am very happy with the SPIRIT OF CHANGE part of this pie." She wrote, JULES, beside SPIRIT OF CHANGE. "I'm beginning to visualize the Venn diagram idea. Do you remember that class? John Venn was a mathematician who developed the idea of relations between a collection of sets."

Everyone grabbed their notebooks and opened to a blank page. "Like this?" Sara opened to scribbles. "I loved the Venn class; I've been playing already. Last month Jon and I talked about the local housing shortage." She showed her notebook to Jules. Sure enough, those words were in the center, in large letters and circled, then intersected with other circles: vacant lots, tiny houses, remodelers, builders, construction loans, materials [Traders, Home Depot, Franklins, ProX].

Using her two dad's given names comes naturally to Sara. She was adopted by Jon and Dex as a baby through an agency and doesn't know anything about her birth parents. She likes to be clear; she has two dads.

"You have seriously taken advantage of those two guys." Jules started laughing, her first good laugh since her accident. "You make me laugh." She was holding her sides before she could stop. "We're all incredibly lucky. We. I just realized the 'I' is dissolving into 'We.' Ahhh."

But Sara was not done explaining, "The housing shortage has been a major problem in Sandpoint and Bonners Ferry for months. I heard Dad talking with Mayor Shelby about tiny houses, but no one knows how to keep them warm in the winter months." Holding up her page, "This drawing was created before I even knew about Drawdown or the interconnections. Puzzles are so interesting, don't you think?"

Alex began to laugh, "You are off and running and your destiny is showing." The girls had played with astrology in middle school. Sara has a powerful birth chart; it was the only thing that followed her from birth because being adopted she had no heritage story, only a birth certificate from Haiti. With those, the girls created their natal charts.

Looking ahead, they had all shared charts for the 12th of January when Saturn and Pluto would be conjunct. Sara's conjunction exactly conjoined her Part of Fortune in the 12th House. She was under the impression that this destiny point indicated an Old Soul nature inside of her, something that was outside their local culture, maybe closer to New Orleans than Sandpoint. Did she have a Ghost Spirit somewhere down there, near the water? Sara didn't really know where her people were from and she was scared to do 23andMe to find out.

Dot interrupted her off-topic meanderings. "Paul says, this opportunity—

the climate emergency—is perfect feedback from our Earth."

Everyone noticed Dot's new familiarity with Paul Hawken and pulled a face. "Paul?!?"

Dot looked around at three clown faces and stuck out her tongue. "Yes, Paul. We would want to do all of the Solutions anyway." Dot tugged on the hat she always wore and drew out each of her words. "And we had better get busy because it is going to happen anyway. Lots of things. My mom says this all the time. Lots of things are going to happen."

Dot leaned over Sara's drawing. The facing page in Sara's big notebook showed a Venn diagram of intersecting circles: food, jobs, schools, emergency supplies, thrift stores. Immigrants from the coastal areas will need more than just housing. "Even before anyone migrates here from Portland," she explained, "we already have a homeless problem. Dex says the folks at our soup kitchens are really the only locals who know how to welcome new people coming to settle here. As a community, we need to be clear about the help we can offer.

"Technically, anyone who moves away from the coasts or tornado alley will be a climate refugee. Did you know, we have families who came here after Hurricanes Katrina and Harvey and stayed? I will interview Mayor Shelby about his plans."

"That's inspiring, Sara," Dot said. "I want to play." She drew a large circle and wrote Ag-Gardening in the center. Feeling a bit like a teacher, she gave everyone a twinkle eye, as she wrote across the top, REGENERATION. "This is what the Earth does perfectly well without our interference. We learned about photosynthesis in the 5th grade, remember? So, when we interfere ..." She began filling in other circles; she spoke as she drew: "Agriculture-Gardening, Grazing, 4-H, Stopping Development ... I have lots of incomplete thoughts. Are we planning to interfere with Earth's systems in any way?"

Jules offered a word. "Write down Plowing—you'll meet lots of farmers who plow up their fields. As far as I can tell, none of the Solutions would be considered interference, only cascading benefits. I heard Paul Hawken say this, and I still don't know what it means. Exactly."

"Whoa, look at that," Dot said, turning to Sara and Alex, "We already need workers to restore farmland, to rehabilitate buildings to live in. This means jobs! Who can give us the economics lesson for our new paradigm? Do you remember when Mason was flush because her two moms were planning to rehab buildings in Detroit? She told me that's what they are doing in New Orleans now. Let's find and rehab abandoned buildings before we build new housing." For her last circle, Dot wrote, Business-as-usual and drew a big line across it.

"Think a little deeper: What does this mean to our businesses, to our town? Try to figure out what must change—transform that to become something else planet-friendly. Let's make us a list—cascading benefits on one side and what needs to go away on the other side."

Suddenly, Jules remembered what Gail had said on one of their Zooms, as though she was planting a seed. "She asked me to visualize my closet. The clothes I refuse to wear could be remade. When I told her that clothes do not interest me, she made a funny face. I reminded her I am a science nerd and she laughed and said she couldn't help herself. Teens have stereotypes like people see elders with canes.

"She texted me a book cover. I found it right here on the New Books shelf, so it's my next read." Straight out of her bag she pulled *Burn: Using Fire to Save the Planet*. "The idea of biochar will make us money right here and make everything greener. Slash piles will never be burned like last fall, not ever again. I want to ask the county commissioners to write a resolution. So many ideas! Who's our note taker?"

Sara raised her hand. "I've got my recorder on. When I get home, I 'll translate to Word and highlight our reminders." She had polished this skillset from the Storytelling Workshop.

Alex turned to Jules. "OK, smarty pants. See how you've directed the show from a bed and a chair? Since you have browsed the whole book ahead of everyone else, show us your Venns." Jules blushed because she was feeling smart. Their Project was how she was going to heal her leg.

They talked over an hour off-topic. "I remembered my 8th grade English project. Gail said it reminded her of a comparative religion class she had taken. The success of our efforts totally depends on people's beliefs. This is really hard." She looked at Sara, her ally on this subject. "Christians have been slow to evolve their view of the Earth's bounty, especially the part about God putting everything here for man to use. That won't matter a wit." Smiling, she recognized one of Gran's famous idioms.

"The great thing about this slice of our Project, we get to research all of the mini-communities already here. Each church, the non-profits, even the PTOs, they all offer an essential piece to the community, like a Spirit. Each one provides a different flavor. Each human offers human energies: We will come together like ingredients in a good soup; we need Dex to help us!" Jules turned to Sara who was surprised to hear her dad's name. Dex was a former biker dude, with tats on every inch of his upper torso. His particular destiny was cooking; he's the chef at three different restaurants and he's famous for raising money for the five soup kitchens in town.

Jules wiggled and admitted, "I don't know much beyond that and won't be getting too much into religion. Just look around—we have a Pagan, a Catholic, a Jew and two generic Christians turned Nones. These are the ingredients for Spirit Soup, right? Me? I'm into new ways of being with Earth as a living organism."

Pointing to the last on the list, Jules said, "Gail is left with another really hard part, Rights of Nature." She wrote GAIL next to the heading. "Gail chose this to give lawful rights to Mother Nature, all that we take for granted: Mountains, Lakes, Rivers, Trees. She's all about giving local legal rights to these things. She said a massive movement has begun around the world, indicating she already had a support network. She said, each sector will be equally hard."

"There's more," Jules continued gleefully. "Gail knows a couple of women here who can help me with the timeline. I was surprised to hear how long Sandpoint has been working on climate change adaptation. I will talk with Nancy Gilliam and the Gerth sisters, Jean and Nancy, from *350Sandpoint.org*. I'm really excited that Gail could offer this much history."

For a year these four friends had discussed the worldwide protests, how change might come to the place they called home, and how their wildlife encounters might change. Jules was tired but had one more thought. "If Rights of Nature was a local law already in place, our big beautiful Lake Pend Oreille would have more protection than it does. Maybe it's not too late to stop the second rail-bridge across to Hope. The river would be protected from the smelter, too.

Every part of the living Earth would have more rights."

Chapter 4

TO THE HEART OF THE MATTER OF DRAWDOWN

Aweek passed. Everyone experienced a super intense weekend. Two Project Scholars on the team went to the obligatory first meeting with the Dean. Sara and Alex were a little frustrated when they tried to explain their Project to their Dean of STEM and were told that their scattered approach may not work.

"She really said that, 'scattered approach,'" Alex explained to Jules who had to stay home with a fever. The girls had all come to Jules' house for their meeting. Jules' had meant to officially introduce Gail who watched the girls interact. She said she would be their "Coyote Mentor," as she described her role to her parents who shared a little history with Gail from the school garden project. Students led their own science project. Gail's role would unfold through asking good questions. She knew the Drawdown website had captivated the girls for the past week.

"I have leaked information," Dot said. "The other girls' team is working on the migration of our elders to winter camps along the Mexican border. That seems important right now. I would love to have my grandparents' attention like you have Gran. Think of all they know. I'm going to ask them to text me answers to my questions. They split the family this time of year when they escape from the cold. Mom's parents live half a year in Bali and my other grandparents drive around in their RV looking for warmer weather."

Occupying most of the front room, a hospital bed replaced Jules' cushy bed; she needed the adjustable angles. Now drenched in sunlight, she looked a bit angelic. She was actually feeling more like a Scholar every day. Her fever had spiked several times, up then back down. Her surgeon specifically requested that Jules not move, so a nurse inserted a catheter and hung a pee bag off to the side.

"The Solutions are laid out in sectors," Jules explained. "I made you all copies of these introductory pages." She handed out the copies and gave a twinkle eye to Gail, mouthing, "Thank you."

"Food seems like the easiest subject, but like Mom said, actually hard as hell. Here in our privileged part of the world, all people eat three times a day, but according to the top Solution on food, food waste is considered an acceptable pattern in restaurants, schools, and hospitals. Even the growers at our own farmers' markets are food wasters, but at least they take produce home and recycle it in their compost pile."

Jules held up her notebook. FOOD in the center circle was intersected by five other circles. "A little sloppy, but you can see this as the supply chain for food: Prep the soil, obtain seeds, plant and water. Through practices associated with REGENERATION," pointing her notebook toward Dot, "a soft layer of cover crops permanently and completely covers any bare soil." She scratched her leg under her cast and winced, "Oooo, that hurt. Harvest – cool – deliver. This can be a short supply chain or a long one. Think about artichokes."

Everyone swooned. Jules didn't. She continued, "Have you ever seen an artichoke grow? They need a very long growing season, something we don't have here in North Idaho. They require so much to get here: machete-effort to pick, refrigeration and packaging, diesel fuel to ship them to a grocery like Yokes or a co-op like Winter Ridge Natural Foods. We probably should enjoy them while we have them. When we get enough sense to stop business-as-usual, this long supply chain—from Chile all the way through Mexico to here—will cease."

Jules pushed a button to lower her butt so she could straighten her spine. "Gail asks us," nodding to the silent figure sitting in a corner chair, closely watching, "what can be done without all that transportation? We've learned about local food from our farmers' markets. Now we need to imagine feeding ourselves and 56,675 people, maybe 60,000 people, 52 weeks a year without shipping in from outside. She calls this *local-local*."

"Hard as hell," Dot said, and they all laughed. Jordi had stacked their camp chairs in the far corner, so the girls settled in and leaned their packs nearby.

"Back to SOLUTIONS," Jules said, turning the page in her art book. "If we pledge to localize our solutions, we can let the transportation sector wait. If you think food is a hard sector, look at this." Protecting Forests was alone in a circle. "We all saw those logging trucks every five minutes going to Coeur d'Alene or Moyie Springs, both directions.

Remember worrying about that?"

Sara kind of raised her hand, "Ya, we went up to Banff and you're right. Every five minutes, a logging truck from here to the border and even crossing the border, trucks going both directions. What is that all about?"

Alex cleared her throat, "Grandad drives one of those cross-Canada trucks. He says he's really busy, there's more logs than they can handle right now. Like our visit to the St. Joe. Whole mountain sides are being cut right here, in our two counties, away from the view-shed all the way up Hwy 95. All we see are the trucks. Grandad was sad at the St. Joe. Maybe he will retire and help me inventory the trees. Maybe my dad will help me talk to other loggers. Ever since I was about nine years old, he has taken me with him to all the secret places here in the Panhandle. It seems like a dream, but I would love someday to take girls into the woods and teach them survival."

Jules said, "See, already we have more Venns. I love that you bring girls into the middle of our circle. When did we stop being girls? The Solution for Educating Girls just made our list."

"O-yay, a prayer has been answered," Alex said, then lowering her drama-meter, "Dad and Grandad will be a big help. No more business-as-usual on logging will create an unemployment crisis right here. Exaggerate that, draw an arc from here to every small mill town all the way to the ocean. There will be some work replanting trees, where do that many baby trees come from?"

Opening her notebook to another page, Alex continued, "I've listed a few Solutions that I want to talk about. "Let's order a pizza and watch a Paul Hawken video, want to?"

Just then Sara's dad, Jon Jewell, knocked lightly and opened the door. He came in with his arms around a stack of books. "How's my timing? I brought you each a gift from the law offices of Powell and Jewell."

Seeing pizza beneath the stack of Drawdown books, Sara exclaimed, "You're reading my mind, doing that telepathy thing again." Her father buried his face in Sara's afro to plant a kiss on the top of her head and passed out books. Gail held out her hand for a shake. "I'm Gail; I'm their mentor," gesturing with a circle motion toward the girls. "Thank you for this generosity, Mr. Jewell."

"Please call me Jon. I've heard lots about you. Where have you been hiding?"

Gail exhaled a sigh, "Long story. For a decade we lived up Grouse Creek. Do you know that area?"

"Are you kidding?" he laughed. "All our senior parties were held at the Falls. Did you own the geodesic dome greenhouse?"

"An amazing guess. Yes. So, you graduated from here. When?"

Sara interrupted, "You two will have to catch up later. We've been talking for two hours and it's been intense. We're going to eat this amazing pizza and watch some YouTube."

Clearly, Sara was in charge.

The following week, Gail stepped into the school study room with her arms wrapped around a pizza. Jules had rallied with no fever all week. "Just look all those Venn diagrams," Gail said. "Wow! I'm amazed at what you have been doing. I love smart girls more than anyone on Earth!" She put down the pizza and gave Jules a little cheek-kiss then hugged the others.

Jules raised her voice over the others. "So, tell us Gail, where have you been? We started an hour ago."

"Well, the pizza took 20 minutes and I went shopping before that!" She sent a twinkle eye straight into Jules, smiled, and set a large colorful candle in the middle of their table. "I hope it's alright to light this here because I am going to." With a little trouble and three matches, she lit the three wicks. "Beautiful girls, please put down your notebooks and pens and close your eyes.

"I bring ceremony to include Great Spirit and our Guides into our conversation. This is not for religious purposes at all. I received some training I want to share with you—Pranayama breathing practice. It can be used to clear your thoughts, especially any self-negatives like doubt and fear. This will give us a blank slate. Our intuition and inner selves will guide the Muse in each one of us. Close your eyes and center your mind on your breath. Breathe in to a 4-count, 1-2-3-4. Hold, 1-2-3-4, and breathe out, 5-6-7-8, long pause. Again. Focus on your breath. In-out. In-out. In-out. Now open your eyes and make eye contact with each one at the table."

Gail had not taken a chair. Instead, she circled the table like a loving she-cat, a metaphor she enjoyed. After a long pause so everyone could absorb how much Pranayama had changed the energy in the room, Gail asked, "Tell me what's been happening." She took the first slice of pizza and passed around napkins. Soon they were digging in and talking all at once.

With her mouth full, Jules raised her slice. "Yum, so good, thanks Gail. We spent the week with our books as you advised. And, I got out of the bed and back into the chair."

Gail dropped another Venn diagram onto the table. In the center circle she had written the word ME. Then in individual circles connecting and overlapping that center circle, the girls saw the words: Mother, Father, Siblings, Grandmothers, Grandfathers, Friends, Teachers, Mentors.

"Let's bring all these folks into this conversation now, please. New blank page first, draw nine circles and stop there."

While they were working on their circles, Gail cleaned up the pizza box and napkins and went to the fountain with water bottles from everyone. No plastic here. She said to herself, this is grand.

Peering over their shoulders before she sat down, Gail whispered to Sara, "No siblings. That's something special."

Taking a breath, she continued. "You will often hear me say, Zoom-Out, I always want the big picture view. Why would we work so hard? Five women cooperating—this will change your life, you know! Do you see how your efforts will set the stage for our communities to benefit, Sandpoint and Bonners Ferry, even Clark Fork and Priest River? That, my dears, is why we start with your personal concentric circles. I learned this from the man who started the Nature Connection Movement. That is a clue to support your inventories, Alex. When you get to the list of Friendlies, please remember the centers of Nature Connection for kids, especially where overnight camps are offered."

Gail took her notebook, turned the page and showed the girls a carefully drawn concentric circle example illustrating the orbits of ME. "We will pull in many community members by doing these two *love* drawings. All we need to do is include those folks we already love."

Beneath the Saturn-like rings, Gail had listed their 5 Sectors. "This will be how we become weavers for our community. After we overlay our people by Sector, we share with our people how they appear in our Projects. Karen is my example; we have worked together since a little dinner party she threw, maybe back in 2010. Then we worked on Transition Town and a Folk School model. From your personal relationships, ask: Who belongs to a Sector because of a strength? It might be special knowledge or experience, or a passion, like a vocation. Why do you consider them Friendlies? Be detailed enough to include specific Solutions, if you know.

"Work with these lists, soon all the good people you know and love will find their place. Spend time sharing your unique circles with each other. Introduce your family's talents to your friends. Think of this as a harvest.

"I call you *Weavers in the Pranayama*. We wove our breaths together. Like the spider's web design, here's another layer in the weave. See you on Friday," she wiggled her fingers goodbye and went out the door.

TURNING TO ONE ANOTHER

There is no power greater than a community discovering what it cares about.

Ask "What's possible?" not "What's wrong?"

Keep asking.

Notice what you care about.

Assume that many others share your dreams.

Be brave enough to start a conversation that matters.

Talk to people you know.

Talk to people you don't know.

Talk to people you never talk to.

Be intrigued by the differences you hear.

Expect to be surprised.

Invite in everybody who cares to work on what's possible.

Acknowledge that everyone is an expert about something.

Know that creative solutions come from new connections.

Remember, you don't fear people whose story you know.

Real listening always brings people closer together.

Trust that meaningful conversations can change your world.

Rely on human goodness.

Stay together.

~ **Margaret Wheatley**

Chapter 5

SELF-PROFILING WITH VENN CIRCLES

Gail had an idea of taking the girls' bonding to a new level. Jules was confined to bed for her IV drip again and saved Gail a Thai take-out box. Gail held up her big blank journal, so the girls saw where they started on Monday, the blank circle diagrams, Venn style.

Then she turned the page to show another one filled in with many names. Every relationship was arranged by talents specific to their Sectors. "Who wants to go first? Wait! Can I go first?"

"ME: 69 years old. Parents, Fern and Leo, both gone now. Siblings, five, but I am only close to my three younger sibs. My bro is in real estate, well so is my youngest sister, but Michele's real love and talent is Lands. Debbie owns grocery stores, so she's got a Food talent. I'm a Scorpio with Libra Rising. O type blood and a Zero° Aries Moon. There is not another single Soul on Earth with my exact imprint. One of my gifts is for Women and Girls.

"None of you have spouses, but you could sneak in a little circle for romance if you feel the love. I have a big circle for Kenny, my sweet artist, and for Rosie our Doodle. Another big circle for mentors. See how this overlaps to include my closest friends who hold me with love? Foodies crowd the Food sector. They're here because I feel their love in return. In the mentor circle so many influences emerged: some of those have died. My grandparents, all five of them were gone when I was 34. Wow, half my life ago. Their influence still comes around regularly, you'll see that when I talk about them. My parents crossed over in 2001 and 2002.

"Who are your life relationships? Who do you cover with your love? I've included my Women's Circles, my Initiation Circles and all the storeowners I know, like growers here in the outer layer. Farther out, the Sacred-Others, the wild animals I have sighted and my pet friends. This last circle will help me with Rights of Nature. We invoke their Spirits through memory.

"First," holding up her finger for drama, "does anyone need a bathroom break besides me?"

When Gail returned, Sara raised her hand. "I want to do another candle-light session for both drawings, I love that Venns are not the only way to de-scribe ME: 16 years old, Mother Dexter and Father Jon, that's really personal, you know. We only know my birthday, but nothing else. June 21, 2003 = high summer and solstice birthday parties. Year of the Water Goat. No siblings that I know of, teachers yes, I have loved a few in the last ten years. Friends have been the center focus of my love since I'm an only child. Possibly Filipina or Hai-tian, definitely fat." Nodding to her pals, "You all survived the mean-girl phase; many of the girls I know didn't make it into my circle of love. No boyfriend, I think boys are yucky."

Gail added, "I would guess your blood type is O like mine, but maybe A or B. Find out for emergencies, everyone needs to have theirs on record."

Alex stood up with her notebook. As Junior Class President she is used to making herself visible. "I will do this a few times to get it right, but first ME: 17 in three days. Mother, Deborah, and father, Joe, Jr, newly divorced, four sib-lings, a couple of teachers."

Alex was writing and drawing wildly to keep up with her thoughts. "AB negative. You know about my grandfather Joe from his namesake river down by St. Maries. Grandma Trixie. Joe and Trixie just had their 50th Anniversary, even though they married late in their 20's. Mom's parents already gone, a car accident when I was five. I feel like I have too many friends, if that is possible. Teachers and Mentors seem like the same thing, but there is Perky Hagadon at the top of my list. She loves that my favorite subject is ecology. I haven't thought about this before." Her eyes were shining, and a teardrop fell to the page.

Dot stood up. "I've been sitting the whole day, Urgh! Thank you for this image of love, Gail, it's kinda cool. You know, I remember you from Northside. I only came to the School Garden Project a few times, but the day you came to the cafeteria to share bean soup from the garden was so awesome. I put you in the Mentor circle.

"Here's ME: 17 on March 21. A wilderness girl; before I got Dad's Mustang, I bussed from way up Flume Creek. Siblings, ya, three, all younger. Mother also Dorothy, that's why they call me Dot. Father Jerry, the pilot. My Grandparents all live along Rapid Lightning Creek, half time. I don't have too many friends No boyfriend. I think my favorite mentors, besides Perky, all come from books."

Gail came around and gave Dot a little squeeze, "Mine too! Thank you."

Everyone turned to Jules. "Oh God, I would love to stand-up," stressing her arms on the wheelchair. "Here's ME: 17, parents, Jordi, math teacher and therapist mother, Robin, who will be here in 12 minutes to rescue me. I need to pee. My older sister, Samantha lives large in this circle; she leads the school paper.

"Grandparents own the Western Pleasure Ranch. Dad's parents own a vineyard in Napa Valley." Jules pointed to a little bubble for her boyfriend Devin, smiled and said, "All my other friends are right here around this table.

"As far as teachers, I've loved lots of them, including Gail, when she taught us how to grow food at the Northside School Garden. That was the last year of elementary when I broke my arm, before we moved to town. Mentors must be coming in my future, unless teachers are mentors."

When Jules stopped talking, Gail stood up and suggested they take moments to be silent and welcome all these relations.

"When you re-graph this, add in all of the townspeople you know. It takes a village, right? Lots of people have added to your upbringing. Remember friends of your parents. I bet you'll love this part!

"For presentable versions of both circles, add in animals as friends and any from the wild you may have encountered or seen."

Gail turned another page in her book showing her concentric circles with animals named all around the outer edge. "Remembering animal sightings reminds me to go wild!"

ENTELECHY

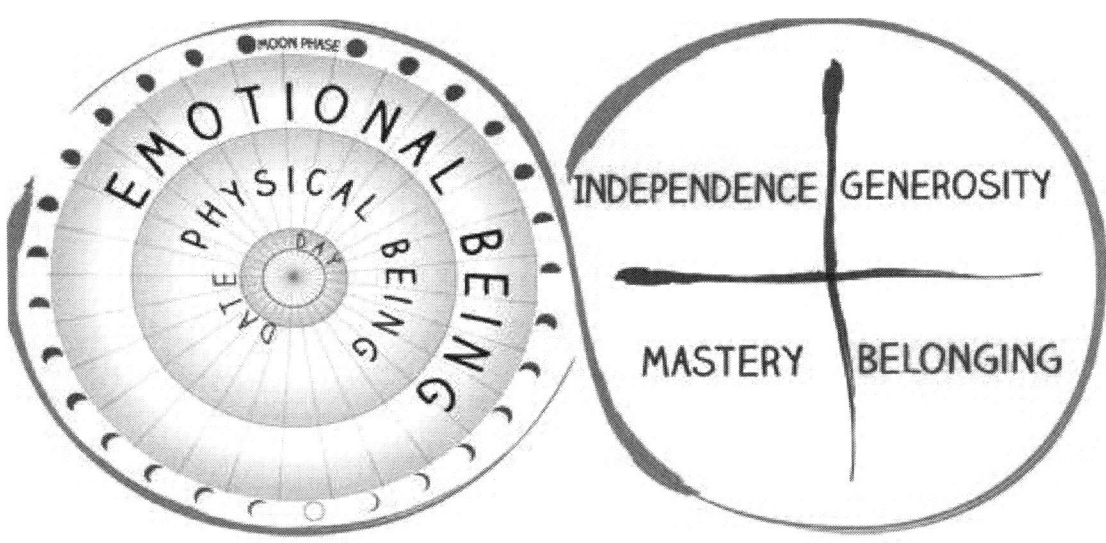

Will you search Circle of Courage (Larry Bentro) to learn the deeper meaning here? Do you know interdependence is the way from talent to entelechy? It takes a village.
Do you know how your moods change with your bleeding cycle?

Let's go a little deeper into personal development. I'm offering you this handout with no explanation. See what you can discover on your own. Send me your questions by email.

Robin flung open the door and the energy changed. Jules said, "Straight to the bathroom, please." Calling over her shoulder, "When is our next meeting?"

"How about Friday?" Sara suggested. "Should we ski and then come here?" Sara was thinking on her feet. They could take the Mustang up the mountain for a few runs of skiing and then to Jules' house by one o'clock. "We'll begin somewhere TBD; we thought we should examine the lists of Solutions."

Dot blew out the three wicks on the big candle and with a little spit-pinch minimized the smoke. Gail hung around to say goodbye to Robin. It really had been a long meeting.

In this mythical time of planetary emergencies, women remember we thrive in small communities. Introducing a paradox: This is climate fiction, but climate is not fiction. Small communitities and local-local actions will be the only way to steer the corrections for our Mother Ship.

~ **Gail Burkett**

They had been holding team meetings during a long, last class on the odd days. When Friday arrived, they opted for another sleepover, Dot with Alex at her mom's and Sara at Jules'.

Gail announced, "Tomorrow is February 1st, Imbolc, the half-way point between Winter Solstice and the Spring Equinox. Did you know it's been celebrated since pre-Christian days?" She invited her she-cat image again, prowling around Pergosi's living room card table. "I'm only here for a little while, so my Dearhearts, let's set the stage, shall we?

"What Paul Hawken said is true: We need to do all of the Solutions for this Project to work long term. By 2050, you'll all be middle-aged and feeling so happy that you helped pull the Industrial Age back from the brink of destruction." Gail realized these young women had not thought much about life beyond this Project.

Jules was feeling crystal clear about Drawdown, completing her second read through. She was back on pain pills, but maybe they enhanced her daydreaming. The Scholars had texted her about being able to think beyond mere sentences into more complex thoughts, closer to paragraph length; she seemed to always have one more paragraph to add.

They made sandwiches and brought cupcakes, now decorating the little round table. Jules wanted to be a thoughtful hostess, so she asked about drinks while she lit their candle. "It's my birthday weekend." Balloons were tied to the corner of her empty bed. Quickly, she jumped in ahead of Gail's next thought. "Anyway, Paul meant worldwide for the 100 Solutions, didn't he?" She picked up her academic paper and read, "Locally, some Solutions are more appropriate than others," and ad-libbing, "some of them are freakin' obvious."

Jules continued reading from her paper: "When they are considered appropriate to our ecosystems, we will inherently see how to expand each individual Solution as a measurable presence in the bioregion. Solutions help us in two directions: They reveal how to protect carbon that is here or how to draw down carbon to store in the soil through the plants. Solutions currently working here, like our beautiful forests, will definitely be easier to understand and expand to scale. Our familial circles will transform into the collective. We will not be doing any of these Solutions alone."

She stopped reading but continued from her notes. "Now for the inquiry: We will ask our questions until answers emerge. These are Level 2 questions, beyond the personal: How can we get 56,675 people to cooperate and collaborate with every other living being in these two counties? How can Drawdown for the Kootenai Bioregion be pared back to one or two Solutions in our four chosen Sectors? We feel ambitious but we would love to do a few Solutions really well. Deep wisdom and systems-thinking in the greater community will help inform our decisions."

Gail gave Jules a twinkle-eye and passed out three sheets of paper that listed, grouped and defined the 100 Solutions from *Drawdown: The Most Comprehensive Plan Ever Proposed to Reverse Global Warming.*

"Wow, this is fantastic," said Jules. "You have so many tools in your toolbox."

Gail led the conversation through one more exercise to narrow their focus. "Ordinarily, these are handed out to groups who sign up for the more advanced Drawdown course. Consider yourselves advanced from this moment forward! To prepare for your orals in May, how many meetings can we have between now and spring break at the end of March?"

Alex said, "I figured that out already."

"I did too," Dot said. They looked at each other. Dot spoke up. "Only eight weeks left, right? If we get more intense in February than we were this month, we can complete two meetings each week, that's 16 meetings. Two late busses home for me unless I drive."

Jules felt like she was interrupting but insisted, "That feels like way too much for this month of writing. Aren't you ready to draw your Solutions and get busy writing? I am. Look how deeply we penetrated our topics already. Do you benefit from solo research time like I do?"

Sara touched Jules hand and looked her in the eye. "That's an obvious question. You have the most sense of anyone I know, but are you ready to limit yourself?"

Jules sighed. "Physically, I am already exhausted but scholastically, I've never felt more turned on. Can I just say *maybe* if I learn some time-management?"

Gail pushed the lit candle into the center of the table. "Right. Let's do our opening. Who remembers?"

Alex raised her hand to volunteer. "Wiggle into your Sitz Bones, Scholars. Put down your books and pens and close your eyes. Breathe in through your fingers to a count of 4 and out through your toes to another 4." In. Out. In. Out. Two more times in silence.

Gail sat with the young Scholars to breathe. By the time everyone opened their eyes, she was wiping away tears.

"I'll submit the name of our Project as soon as we agree," Sara said. "How about Solution Scholars? Do you like the use of SS, the alliteration?"

Dot pulled back her long red hair and held it with a scrunchy at her neck. "Do you like that better than Drawdown Scholars?"

Gail blew her nose. "Vote." They settled on Drawdown Scholars, for the pointed clarity. Sara acted as if she was their leader. "Can I be Team Captain? I'm already totally involved with my dad on this Project. And I already reported—tried to report—to Dean Yost. I'm glad I have easy subjects this quarter."

Everyone looked at Sara. Alex said, "I feel so lucky that you want to." Dot said, "I have too many chores."

"I have this other thing to deal with," Jules said. "Hey, the cast came off on Wednesday. The bummer is the Doc found MRSA, and he wants me to stay still again. It really sucks. Hey, we could do another research project on super-bugs." Jules tried to laugh off her bad news, "If Dr. Jim keeps putting me through X-rays, I might turn into a bionic woman before we're finished."

Gail frowned. "That's not really funny. I guess you already know how serious MRSA is. So sorry dear. You can beat it, but you must put heart and soul into doing just that. We'll talk after I check in on Robin's analysis." Gail examined the IV antibiotic drip bag of dalbavancin. "It may be harder now to focus for all of you." Jules reached for a Kleenex and wiped her tears.

She leaned into one of the only whines anyone ever heard from her. "Less than a month in that cast and my leg came out infected. My mom said MRSA is all too common in hospitals, even great ones like Sacred Heart. All things simultaneous, right Gail, haven't you told us that?"

Gail didn't let go of Jules' hand. "Let's vote on Team Captain and then decide what all things simultaneous means."

Aye. Aye. Aye. Aye. "Four ayes," Sara bowed. "I humbly accept your vote of confidence."

Jules pulled a funny face and said, "Humbly?" Everyone laughed.

"I think Team Captain supports self-confidence and helps me with personal doldrums," Sara told them. "I've beaten a trail from my house to Jules' ever since the climate marches, remember? We are the generation to fix the messes of all the other generations. Besides, I was your campaign manager," she nodded to Alex. "I learned a few things doing that for you. There are a few regular admin. duties I want to do, like submitting Drawdown Scholars as our project name and reserving a study room at school. Scheduling our orals next quarter will be a big deal. Should we do that soon? What else?"

Gail chimed in, "You have all used time like you were masters, but here it is February already. And, okay, add me to the group text for a little while. I should know about stuff. Sara, you can brainstorm the calendar with me, I can't do that alone. For today ..."

She took out her big journal and opened to the spider web illustration. "I created this from our last meeting. I've been working with these Solutions' lists for a couple of years, right?" Their eyes widened and everyone huddled around to see. Gail laid the drawing flat in front of Jules as the others stood up.

"If you look at your handouts you will see there are too many Solutions and even too many Sectors. This is a Junior Project, remember? We have four Sectors and need to limit our inquiry to two Solutions each, using the spider web to discover cascading benefits.

"I will teach you three things today, maybe you should write this down: 1) scholarly writing starting today; 2) how to mindfully narrow your focus; 3) the top secret to all of your future academics are four little words so you finish your assignment and integrate your learning back into your life. Those words are *document and get out.*"

Here's our academic form: "Write opening paragraphs about your lenses of perception. These four perspectives are most personal already because you chose them early. Notice how easily you can talk about SPIRIT OF CHANGE or BIOREGION stuff. Dot took REGENERATION to a place that Paul Hawken didn't even consider, and Sara did the same thing with CLIMATE JUSTICE.

"Credit how much you have learned already by writing about these big topics as your Introduction. Use clarity as your muse. Throughout February, I think ten typed pages of Introduction and Conclusion—yes, these are related, that will do nicely. Remember, *all things simultaneously*. While you're doing that, dive deeper into your Sector, focus on what is real for you. Zero in on the two Solutions that attract you the most. What can you teach the student body?

"At the end of February, let's share and edit each other's writing to clean up the edges and then submit a draft by the end of quarter. We can all take a nice, long spring break!"

The girls looked intently at the spider's web. Feeling the need to be playful, Gail circled the little round table, cat-like, looking directly into Alex's eyes. "BIOREGION and RIGHTS OF NATURE hover in the spirit realm above the land. Own your Sector. Show me what you already know. Which of these Solutions do you find here in our two counties?"

With a twinkling eye, she pointed to Jules, "This is an example of getting everyone to work with you. Each of you will now choose specific Solutions, run right on down this list. Mark the ones that probably are here in our bioregion. You have already chosen your perspectives. On this spider's web note down Solutions in our two counties from these Sectors. Take your time."

Gail handed out two pages of the spider's web to practice on. "Let's see if this is a useful tool, okay? Then at the end, like a gift, we will each choose the one or two to present in depth to our community. Don't forget, we see the whole picture like architects, keeping the end of this Project in our hearts and minds.

"Notice the intersection between your brain and your heart. Which Solutions have been under our noses already?"

Silence fell as the girls studied the 100 Solutions. The candle flickered. They all seemed to hold their breath before Jules said, "We are going to choose today and end the mystery, right? It looks easy enough."

Sara naturally took the lead. "Narrow your focus. Let's use a sticky note and write the Sector we're drawn to first." She passed around a little pad. No one hesitated; they all took a note and quickly wrote something down.

Jules raised her hand. "I'll go first." she put her sticky note that said Food down on a corner. Alex put her sticky note, Women and Girls, on another corner. They all nodded at her, kind of amazed. Dot put her note down on Land Use and Sara, jumping up and twirling around, peeled another note off the pad, and put it down on Materials.

Gail stood up and clapped so the room echoed. "I didn't know that would work so well." She was beaming. "Yay, O-yay!"

Everyone agreed. "Yay, O-yay!" Gail and Jules were left alone while the candle burned. "Your Gran and I talked about your leg being a spiritual test. Consider that you are deep into your Heroine's Journey now, Jules. You do not need to lose this leg, but you will need to integrate your whole self, emotionally and spiritually, into a vision of the future and be the boss of your mind. Listen to your parents' coaching, they have been through a similar Passage together." Gail kissed her hand and looked deeply into her eyes, "You got this, Jules!"

Thoughts flowed through the silent house and Gail allowed them to linger.

46

She thought to herself that it's time to view the *Introduction to Drawdown* movie together. This is the order of things. I love this precious time, but it's going by in a flash already. Everyone seems so earnest, but now we have the company of a superbug. She stifled a groan.

When the team reassembled, Gail suggested that maybe their time would be better spent solo. Jules needed to rest and de-stress if she was going to get the upperhand on her infection.

Traveling through the wrinkle, Gail returned to her little abode and committed another hour to the Project because her research on RIGHTS OF NATURE had started to nag her. How to be thorough with so many topics? She did another mind-map drawing. Perhaps there are too many threads: Polly Higgins, Native Wisdom, Extinction Rebellion, oil and gas drilling, sprawling developments, forest and brush fires, coal and uranium, copper and gold. Green New Deal. Local clear-cuts feel the most immediate. How many critters were displaced to satisfy Asia's demand for logs? This feels closest to her heart of worry. Looking at her drawing, Gail realized finding the international justice work by Polly Higgins on ecocide inaugurated this deep inquiry.

Chapter 6

FALLING IN LOVE WITH SOLUTIONS

The Scholars agreed to a week of writing and scheduled by group text to meet the next Friday at Pergosi's house again. Jules was over glad to see everyone.

"Mom is my total shero. She figured out how to show an internet video on the large screen television; she's here to help Gail." Robin leaned against the doorframe. "Glad to get you going. I wish I could stay and watch this, but I have been called to a special meeting for hospital staff on emergency pre-paredness. I support your Project. Jules can share your video with me and Dad later. A cord hooks to your computer, like this, USB to USB and voila, it appears on the screen."

Both rather efficient, Gail was about to turn on her hotspot, but Robin handed her a sticky note with the house's WiFi password. "No need to use up your bandwidth, we're high speed wired." She gave Gail a squeeze and waved to everyone else. Jules blew her a kiss, "Thanks for the popcorn, Mom."

"Everyone, snuggle into your deck chairs," Gail said. "This is interactive, so please get your notebooks and pens." Lighting a candle before beginning each meeting was now their regular ritual. Gail pulled a tiny battery-operated mock candle out of her computer bag and found space on Jules' tiny bed shelf. "Here's our pretend candle," she said. "Who's opening today?"

Dot leaned forward. "Let's say a little prayer for Jules and begin with our breath. We can enjoy the silence while we weave our breath together."

"Okay, open your eyes now, Scholars." Gail held two pens above the arm of her chair. "Now for the drumroll: This *Introduction to Drawdown* takes about 2 hours to run through. I will keep it going and pause it long enough for you to read my personal answers on the screen and write down your own."

After a month of poking at the edges, their Project had begun.

At the top of the second hour, Sara called a break. Gail knew they were more than half-way through but didn't protest. She needed a rest too. At that moment Jules' sister Samantha appeared in the doorway. "Hello everyone. I'm here to help Jules to her bathroom break. Take 10 or 12 minutes for your break, that's how long it takes us."

They put a metal brace around Jules' whole leg; it was cool the way it wrapped and snapped. Holding her under the arms, Sam slid Jules off the cushions and onto the wheelchair. "Easy-peasy," she said.

Dot stepped up to the IV drip. "I got this. Staying overnight last night showed me how to be useful."

They disappeared into the master bathroom around the corner. Gail vigorously rubbed her head, messing up her hair, "This is me de-stressing. I've had a lot of injuries and too many surgeries. Jules laying there so needy feels a little like PTSD for me. I remember being an invalid for a couple of months and needing Kenny's help to do so many things. He used to say, if you broke your leg, I would have sent you home to your mother. Of course, he didn't mean that. It was just a joke because I broke everything but my legs. Destiny brought us together, love and kindness make it easy to stay together."

After the movie finished, they took another break and wheeled Jules into the sunny kitchen. Even though it was just 4 pm Pacific time, the sun had already set behind Baldy Mountain. They needed lots more than popcorn for snacks. Dot pulled out a tray of sandwiches. "I made these this morning. Pretty smart, don't you think?"

Gail offered Jon a chair, "We're about to watch the *Introduction to Draw-down* for a second time. The Scholars have decided it's time to show the movie to the middle school science class. Would you like to sit and watch?"

"I would love that," Jon replied. He had stopped by to drop Sara off and was curious. "It means blowing off the gym, but I go often enough."

"Great! Would you and Sara bring over that table? I'm cued up on my laptop, but we need a prop. Does anyone need a bathroom break?" She looked at Jules.

Alex wheeled Jules away. "Ten minutes please." Bathroom chatter must have been funny because they all emerged laughing, including Jules. Everyone was worried about her.

Gail fiddled with her computer trying to find the high school WiFi. Sara told her dad, "Gail said passion has been the driver in her life. We talked about passion coming from the intersection of heart and head."

After the viewing, Jon took a phone call, waved goodbye to Sara, and disappeared like a ghost out the door. She wiggled her fingers as the study room door closed behind him. Almost the next second her phone vibrated. It was Jon. She turned her phone around for her friends to see. His text read, *Thanks,*

Hon. The Introduction to Drawdown was amazing!

Gail had something important to tell the Scholars and began slowly. "My passion is community. You were all born here. In 2006, the year you turned three, Kenny and I migrated up from southern Idaho and crossed the Long Bridge for the first time; it's quite a famous hook for folks seeking a new community. Did you know that? When I was your age, I grew up near the Utah border. My people have been here in Idaho since 1878.

Alex squinted and took off her glasses, "Mine too! I've been hearing about those ancestor stories of the Greats and the Great-Greats, all my life."

Gail reached over and gave Alex's hand a squeeze, "We will compare ancestors' stories, I promise—mine were loggers, too. Hold this simple question, there are 100 answers: What do I feel passionate about?

"Now turn your attention to this *Introduction to Drawdown*. How will it come across to a younger version of you? To adapt to the middle school brain, can you subtract four years?"

The girls remembered the fun they had in 7th grade science class. It seemed important to them to show the movie there as extra credit for the AP kids. They remembered when Perky taught their extra credit classes. She had told them this is where Advance Placement qualifications began. They invited Perky and asked her to choose a time in mid-February when she could come to the middle school.

Sean Lyon was their science teacher. New to the district, he had come to ski and finish writing his novel. Instead, he was happily distracted with his students who were much smarter than he thought they were going to be. When Dot and Alex went to talk with him about showing the Drawdown movie to his class, Sean thought maybe he could get away to ski that day. But probably not. Perky Hagadon was legendary in the school district. The girls wanted to coordinate with her schedule. Initially, this seemed an annoyance to him. Then he became a star.

Perky knew these girls more by reputation now, even though she had taught them and traveled with them. All kids change so much from year to year, especially teens. The science teachers talked about their students, past and present, at district meetings and teacher training days. AP-STEM was itself an honor, but the sixteen juniors were competing for best performance. They had all found the same groove by taking every one of the extra science offerings. Several of those, like the conservation study in Costa Rica, were masterminded by Perky alone.

The teachers in the school district and the Superintendent were talking.

The Juniors' Projects were already the topic of conversation and the four girls known as the Drawdown Scholars had an advantage: their parents and grandparents were bragging them up through the community.

After giving birth to something – 3 or 4 baby Magpies, or a new, titillating idea – a tending comes next. As seen from the trail below, the behavior of these Magpie parents taught me about care. First one then the other entered the nest and disappeared.

The whole Magpie family had a moment of unity and possibility. Then the parents came out and went their own way to find another meal.

This is when Drawdown came through as an epiphany – we have failed to tend. Attend. Give our precious attention to what is in plain sight.

Solutions began as ideas and only need more tending. They are everywhere.

MARGARET MEAD

"A student once asked anthropologist Margaret Mead, "What is the earliest sign of civilization?" The student expected her to say a clay pot, a grinding stone, or maybe a weapon.

Margaret Mead thought for a moment, then she said, "A healed femur."

A femur is the longest bone in the body, linking hip to knee. In societies without the benefits of modern medicine, it takes about six weeks of rest for a fractured femur to heal. A healed femur shows that someone cared for the injured person, did their hunting and gathering, stayed with them, and offered physical protection and human companionship until the injury could mend.

Mead explained that where the law of the jungle—the survival of the fittest—rules, no healed femurs are found. The first sign of civilization is compassion, seen in a healed femur."

Chapter 7

PAYING IT FORWARD:

The showing at the middle school was the first day back after a snow day and after President's Day. Stuck at home for two weeks, Jules was miserable and in pain. Robin wheeled her, IV and all, into the school auditorium. Secretly pleased, Gail watched the way Dot and Sara took charge of the AV equipment. Impressive. The girls – completely digital from birth – had practiced. Alex told Gail they had each seen the *Introduction to Drawdown* from the Pachamama site several times.

Mr. Lyon opened the door for his students who had stayed after school for extra science credit. Perky stood just inside the door as they filed in and said hello to each one. There were thirteen, a good size group. Alex took the mic. "Welcome," she said, and asked everyone to take a seat.

"Our passion for science comes from teachers who love science. The four of us extend a welcome to you 7th grade climate scientists who stayed today for extra credit. You won't be sorry about staying at school today. A special thank you, Ms. Hagadon." Perky, standing with Robin behind Jules' chair, went up to the front as Alex introduced her. "It is an honor to show you what we have found for our STEM-AP Project this year."

In the darkened auditorium, Gail saw Robin wipe her tears; she was going through rolling emotions as Jules struggled. Theirs had been an intense battle with a super-bug. It was tough to get Jules out of the house now. She wanted Jules to have a full experience, but her present dangerous health crisis meant that was no longer possible. They had to save her leg and save her sanity, too. The only class that didn't suffer was this one, the AP-Project.

Just before Alex started the movie, with its intro by Tracy Apple, the Pachamama Alliance Director of Educational Content for the Drawdown pilot program, Gail noticed someone slide silently through the door, someone she did not know. Quietly, like a cat, Gail went over to introduce herself and saw a press pass hanging around her neck. It was a reporter from the Reader. Gail offered a welcome and pointed to the stage, "Maybe we can visit afterwards?"

The presentation went long, and three kids had to leave to catch the late bus. None of the other ten moved; they were solid to the end. It was a good thing this was a Wednesday, their early-out day. The town kids would still be home before dark. Rides were quickly arranged before Q & A began.

Sara was ready. "We call ourselves Drawdown Scholars. This gathering of knowledge about climate and community serves self and planet. We have learned a lot but only know a little bit: This is true in all sciences. Ask away."

The reporter jumped up. "I graduated a decade ago. How old is this AP-STEM Project for juniors?"

Perky answered, "This is the third of four experimental years. Then the District will evaluate successes. I will vote success!"

Sara laughed. "That was a good question that we don't have the answer to. Thanks. Let's see if the student audience has questions."

One arm shot up, "Now what?" Jennifer asked. The climate marches had brought students together for sign making parties. Jennifer was the artist who added local wildlife drawings and made everyone's sign a keeper. Science teachers gathered them for an art exhibit and Jennifer was the star.

Alex reached for the mic. "Hi Jennifer. We have our own timeline for de-liverables. We still need to write up what we've learned and get ready for our formal Project presentations in May. Those are the minimum requirements. Thanks for coming today and for staying. This was fun to schedule and plan. Step one and done," she beamed at her own poetry. "We could put you on our Team. Do you want to help?"

Jules spoke up, feeling proud of her teammates. "Calm minds prevail. We can give you lists of Solutions in handout form and Mr. Lyons said he will ad-just his curriculum a little bit to talk about Solutions closer to home. Each of you has a new Chromebook, right? Talk to your families. Do your own research and come watch our Project orals."

Knowing they were not going to stay in teacher mode, Alex suddenly felt an adrenalin drain, a sense of overwhelm. To the rescue, Dot reached for the mic. "We've been totally amazed by this very big topic." She held up the book again. "More than 250 scientists poured their hearts and minds into this work. Sorry, that we have only ten more minutes for questions."

Gail wiggled down into a seat, this was wonderful. She gave a little fin-ger wave to Perky two seats over, who had also been watching carefully. They shared a moment of eye contact. All their history melted into a luscious pile with that look. Only a small circle of friends had watched when Gail shifted gears in 2016, dismantling her life in the Panhandle. Those were awkward days, but that's another story. Today, midweek after President's Day and mid-winter, the beautiful warm memory of their school garden project flooded back to her; those were the seeds that had been planted for climate action.

Mr. Lyons peeked at Sara's list of Solutions. "Take a look," Sara encouraged. "We started with the book about Drawdown before we saw these two lists and before we ever saw the movie. The lists create a foundation to choose from because we can't do all 100 Solutions. After we finish our research, we want to present a handful of Solutions that can be scaled up. I'll email digital copies for your whole class."

A student bursting with energy stood up. "So, okay, we saw the movie, we saw the Solutions on a list, but I'm with Jennifer, what's next?'"

Jules still had the mic. "I've been pretty laid up for a month and I've asked myself that same question a hundred times. You and Jennifer each sense an urgent energy that I relate to," Jules continued. "Maybe you've talked about global warming in class, maybe with your friends and family. This is the first place to start.

"We have a new decade. Talk about reversing global warming with every-one. Spend time on the website *Drawdown.org*. Do your own research. Learn something new or find out more about what you already know. Study the Sectors. *Drawdown.org* offers the door, only you can open it. Get ready to be surprised."

Jules was tired and in pain, but she reached out for her Drawdown book that Dot was holding. Jules hadn't planned for questions and wanted to go home, but she waved the book with its fifty colorful stickers poking from the edges and the top. "This came to me the day after Christmas. You can browse through the Sectors online; this whole book is there at *Drawdown.org*. Maybe one or two Solutions will come to you in your dreams. That's what happened to me."

Turning to her teammates, Jules asked, "What's your favorite Solution for this bioregion, Alex?"

Alex did not hesitate. "I love that Educating Girls and Reproductive Rights for Women are – when added together – the #1 Solution to global warming. Let's lift ourselves up. We're just kids but we can lift ourselves up." She sound-ed like a cross between cheerleader and junior class president.

She handed the mic back to Jules who added, "Food is a very big sector and easy to obsess over. Take food waste, one of my new pet peeves; I go hunting in the back of the fridge for waste and find genuine science projects in there." Everyone in the audience laughed.

The science teacher, Mr. Lyons, addressed the students. "Looks like we have begun our journey with Drawdown. You kids are the only ones in Sand-point to see the movie so far. I'll give you each twenty extra points if you write one paragraph before end of class on Friday. Next week we will show the movie to the whole class, and you can be up front answering questions." Everyone stood up and reached for their backpacks.

Perky faced the rustling kids. "I feel like celebrating," then she passed around a tray of chocolate brownie bits. "I'd like to watch the movie again, and I want to see the lists, too. Will you keep me posted on Project progress?"

Amid auditorium chaos, the Reader reporter asked for the mic. "One last question. We met Tracy Apple and Paul Hawken in the movie. How many others are working on this Drawdown right now?"

Jules looked at Dot and quick as a wink, Sara stood up. "We want to acknowledge our mentor, Gail Burkett. She says we are the stars of the show, but she is our secret guide for this Junior Project."

Gail was on her feet already. She came around Perky and squeezed her hand. "Many people have a thread in this tapestry. Now all of you have your own thread. If you've ever seen a story quilt or one of the Navajo tapestries, you will know a simple organizing principle: Warp strings are laid down so that the colorful threads of the weft can create a design. Choose your color.

"We are indeed in a new decade. Pachamama Alliance has an online teaching forum where they offer courses and a place for members to meet—60, maybe 70 communities around the world share this Introduction. The next training is a 5-part workshop. Yes, the whole planet is involved and now Sand-point and Bonners Ferry are on the map!"

She paused as the students enjoyed their chocolate nibbles. "This is the community seed I am planting today: We need to talk, plan, and talk some more. Dream a little and share what you learn from the Drawdown website. Introduce Drawdown to your parents and grandparents, siblings and class-mates. That is precisely where our Drawdown Scholars started. We will form a community that you can join, probably before school lets out.

"Any last words? Thank you for all your good questions." She flipped off the mic and began to coil the cord. Jules sister, Samantha, had been waiting for ten minutes; she came up to the stage to wheel Jules to the car.

"I think everyone is coming over," Gail said. "I texted our order, so I need to pick up Thai take-out first. We are going to debrief together right?"

Right. Everyone knew that was the plan. To Perky Hagadon, Gail said, "You are the seed-planter who we will honor at all our presentations. You made certain these girls had choices. Look how well they chose!" Gail and Perky hugged, they were beaming with pride.

Still smiling, Perky turned to Mr. Lyons. "Good job inspiring your students to get here."

"Does anyone absolutely need a ride?" Gail asked. The students all said no in unison. One boy joked over his shoulder, going out the door, "We'll do a sidewalk debrief on the way to the library. That's where we meet our rides." Gail calculated: the walk was five city blocks, about seven minutes from door to door. Easy to navigate, she thought, even in the snow and cold, because these were North Idaho kids.

Wherever you go, take love with you.
Have you ever wondered about heart stones?
This is Earth Mother loving us, wherever we go, love is there.

Gail put down her chopsticks, still feeling the sting of hot peppers. "I have to catch my ride to Bonners Ferry." No one thought of Gail as a commuter, because she usually simply disappeared. "Will you put one word into the air that best describes for you the experience we had at the middle school?"

Jules was feeling better, the Percodan was kicking in. She knew her word: "Launch!"

"Community!" Alex shouted. This surprised each one of them. "I just got that today."

Dot and Sara smiled at one another. "Rotten!" They said at the very same time. Sara laughed, "Decompose! Maybe we are going to talk about food waste with the community. We're launched!"

Gail wanted to harvest this delightful feeling of elation. "You've launched your Project like a test balloon into the community. Each of those who viewed the movie have concentric circles of relations. We said talk is the next step. They will be talking. I know you are happy, motivated and determined. I am too. What would you like to build on after today?"

Talking over one another's words, Dot punched the air. "We're going to be rock stars!"

A little too loudly, Jules said, "A dog and pony show," something she remembered from one of Gail's New York stories.

Alex muted everyone. "Not so fast—we may fail a couple of times. This is going to be hard."

Sara said, "Ya, if this was easy, people would be doing Drawdown already."

"Great! Soak up these early signs of your genius: Stay with today's happy feelings! Let's begin to discover in this spectacular place we live, where Solutions are already occurring. I'll see you in a week. I've got places to go, people to see, things to do."

Gail got sick, so she skipped over a second week. Each one of the Drawdown Scholars sent her emails every day, suddenly they loved emails. Gail was achy in her bones and depressed. Scientists were reporting their findings about acceleration: Everything that was positively doable in 30 years, needed to be done in half that time, or less. Sea levels were rising measurably. A virus more contagious and more lethal than the flu was surfacing as a global distraction. Gail hoped the old saying was true—It's often darkest before the dawn.

Dex took a trip to Portland, reported what he saw to Sara and shared the information in an email with Gail: At high tide, Portland looked like it was about to flood. One of the accelerants of global warming is methane. The methane thawing in the Arctic and methane not burned off at fracking wells all over the U.S. are changing the game.

Climate scientists depended on computer models for their forecasts. Methane as an accelerant was probably the wildcard of the past three or four extremely hot years, the hottest on record. In the middle of their summer, Australia broke records every day for a month. Those Aussie headlines tore at everyone's heart and woke up millions around the world. When would those fires stop burning?

Gail wrote back, "Now report some good news, would you? There's plenty of that too. Double dog dare."

Sick in bed with her computer, Gail read abstracts, mostly from scientific journals. The next ten years—this is what the wise ones were saying. Her last connection to academia had been Prescott College, a lifetime ago. She tried not to cough and cheered herself up with mentoring memories as she pulled astrology charts for her Drawdown Scholars, kind of like visiting spirit to spirit.

She sent rough drawings of Sectors and Solutions to Laura, Queen of Graphic Design: No other place on the planet looked exactly like their North Idaho place.

Each one of the girls had their own password for the Global Commons. International law identifies four global commons: The High Seas; the Atmosphere; Antarctica; and, Outer Space. Gail knew her Drawdown Scholars would discover this toolbox. She waited ten days.

Dot wrote first. "I found your toolbox!"

Gail wrote back, "Share it around. Maybe our ultimate Game-On Challenge will be showing this to our local politicians. When high school and college students in Kansas City walked out of classrooms at 11 o'clock, Friday, September 20, 2018 they made a challenge to the local governing entities—address climate change. Now we are."

Gail lay back on her pillow and smiled. She had planted two seeds at once. That metaphor was proving quite useful.

Chapter 8
RETURN TO THE ROOT

Jules could do without the drama. She loved doing the research and was spurred on by her teammates. She had her own inner fire burning and needed to understand her long relationship with the tree root that tripped her. A beautiful childhood, this was her recollection. She realized how weird it was for her to be nostalgic about her childhood and simultaneously acknowledge how life would be entirely different if she lost her leg.

Throughout her little-girl years, that gnarled and protruding root had been her stage. Usually Samantha joined in her fun. They played with tiny cowboy and Indian toy pieces, then switched to Barbie dolls. "The Root" was also their stage for dramatic performances; adults would bring camp chairs, sit around and enjoy the show. Dress-up was their dramatic choice through middle school and they performed made-up stories like Disney movies; musicals were their favorites. The Root had rested alone for the past four years, with little drama to celebrate its existence.

Jules mostly stayed in her hospital bed in the front room of her cozy house. Gran set up a cot next to Jules and slept over whenever she could. One morning she woke and found Jules already writing. Jules could see Gran rolling in the sleeping bag, waking herself up, "It's a bit drafty next to that window" she grumbled. "Kinda like my downstairs before the fire gets going."

"Good morning Gran. Do you want to see what I'm writing?"

"Right after I return from the bathroom." She wrapped her arms around a bundle of clothes and returned in a few minutes dressed for the weather outside.

Jules had named her IV drip, Zorro, because it rescued her with antibiotics and pain relief. First thing Gran did was change the drip bag. The pharmacy prepared a special drip mix to fight the MRSA, but Jules was not responding. Robin said it was because this strain was a particularly nasty hospital bug.

Jules reached for her phone to pull up a couple of photos. "I dreamed about the Root, Gran; it looks even more contorted below ground." Gran looked over her shoulder: Images of the Root, taken on a dozen different days since Jules got her phone, archived in her favorites.

Looking straight into her grandmother's eyes, she asked, "Maybe the attraction is mutual. Do you think the Root loves me back?"

Jules began writing poetry to the tree. Gran was filled with gratitude because she knew the spiritual feeling of coincidence growing within Jules. Jules was grappling with a serious situation for any young woman. The doctors had explained the problem to her parents: Without the artificial bone, they would not have tried to save Jules' leg. They may not be able to yet.

Scooching on top of the covers to sit on the bed near Jules good side, Gran read the poem on the laptop and said, "A wise woman deeply ponders her change agent. The Root is your change agent. We could invite my friend Karie to visit with you. Karie is a shamanic practitioner. Would you like that?

"Do you remember on the first day back to school when I said this is your Rites of Passage? Karie understands that a woman's journey is also infused with her personal stories of spiritual coincidences. She led a journey for me once. I would love for her to read the poetry opening out of you like a flower."

Nodding, Jules hit the print button. She handed Gran the sheet with three neat stanzas:

Purpose

The Root of my demise, dear friends, comes with a tree attached
So down-down-down we go to peer into the future according to Tree.
She comes from good stock and has watched 180 years carefully
Tree named Pseudotsuga (Douglas-fir), loyal to North Idaho, she tells
Secrets to me, middle of the night, middle of day, it matters not
Tree reveals water events, historic dangers of fire and windstorms
Each altering our region with a faint imprint of power, weather power
Now the Earth will have her turn, this is what Tree tells me in dreamtime.

Imagine, it's entertaining to imagine how Tree holds so much history
Come with me down-down-down into her roots and become observant
Mystery and purpose live way down here where mycelium rules
Where ancient wisdom for spiritual beings speak through intuition
Tell the truth, have you ever been on a Journey solely to listen?
Listen to Tree rising out of Earth, hear truths long forgotten
Being human comes as a gift with time more limited than many Trees,
Primary instructions arrive through the silence, we live inside out.

Like any seed that sprouts roots, humans arrive as seeds with legs
Most of us are not well-trained, old women hold back wisdom
Tree speaks clearly—Teens can and do change their grandmothers
Maybe the Earth is troubled because Trees became commodities
Old women's wisdom hold human mythology not to be buried
Truth waits for the request: Step right up girls, ask your grandmothers
They will guide our Journey to help the Earth heal, we need them
When I asked Root if she had more secrets, this message was repeated.

"I have to leave you to your work, Jules. Daydreaming is an important part of your healing right now. Increase your meditation time—bring in light through the crown chakra at the top of your head."

Jules said, "I'm sorry I can't get outside right now!"

"Your Root is buried in snow," Gran gently reminded her. "That's the side of the house where snow slides easily; it's still really deep." Picking up on the spiritual connection with her granddaughter, Gran said, "I am glad you and I have these small slivers of time. I'll be back tomorrow. Are you okay for now? Love you like crazy Jules."

"Love you more, Gran!" She turned in the door to catch the kiss that Jules tossed into the air. This was their special secret sauce.

Jules was especially glad she had given Gran a copy of her poem. A few words changed each time Jules read through it, but the message stayed the same. Now she has enlisted her grandmother's wisdom, those wise energies.

Her computer had been dinging rudely while she said goodbye to Gran. Emails flowed almost continuously, something new from her teammates every day. Like owls, they were most comfortable and smartest in the dark. Jules sent them her morning greetings, then added: "Please don't mind me. I am reading and writing. But here's the other thing—while Gail and I are laid up, you are still meeting at school, right? Please plan a meeting over here—I miss you all so much."

Sara responded with a group text, "Does this mean you want company? You have a serious infection, Jules—we're afraid of it. Aren't you?"

Just then the idea popped into Jules head. She grabbed the phone and texted the group: *I am not infectious in an airborne way, so you are all safe to come over. Can you invite your grandmother? Or, another special woman for a long Friday meeting? They can be witnesses to our first practice video. I would like to lead the meeting. Gathering the generations gathers experience, this feels urgent.* She added extra emojis and hit send.

Then Jules felt anxious. She had initiated something and would need to follow through. She wondered, is this foot-in-mouth? Gail says, "If not now, when? If not us, who?" This calmed her inner spirit.

Karie Lee came over that afternoon and with very little small talk between them, she led Jules on a meditation journey with her Root ally. Karie suggested Jules wait to share the spiritual details. "Save the Root story for your Gran or when you are with your teammates alone. You can claim a hospital-bed vision—everyone will understand. Now that you have invited others, be clear how they can help you, and they will."

Jules wished she had recorded everything that Karie told her. "You have written a poem to your Root ally—more will come, because you are in receiving mode. Spirituality will become the inner anchor for all you girls. With the metaphoric potential for perfect vision this new decade 2020 is filled with light and change. Darkness will come too accentuating the light. Transformation comes through such an injury as yours, a quantum leap into who you are meant to be."

When Karie left, Jules felt the room spin and scribbled notes in her journal for about a minute. She was grateful for a nap. Robin came in to give her a sponge bath and change her sheets and Jules had time to engage with her mom. Usually, Robin was on the fly. There was so much on her plate right now. "Gran arranged for a shamanic practitioner to visit this morning. Karie, do you know her?"

Jules was surprised when Robin said, "Very well. She is my massage therapist. I've done lots of personal work with her, which is probably why I appear 'to be a rock,' as you say. Karie has helped me visualize that because it is what you need the most right now."

"OMG Mom—you're absolutely right! Is this why there are so many rocks around the house? What's the story of the big one by the front door?"

"My friends and I have hiked all of the watersheds in this bioregion, you know. We've been to sacred places where water rushes over rocks in the spring and barely trickles in the autumn." Robin brought in the stone by their front door.

"When we are most tuned into the Earth, she creates a connection. If you look generally at this, it's just a rock. Some might say it's even a cool rock. But if you look deeply, this is a Wisdom Stone, as old as the Earth herself. See? This is the Earth watching us and watching all of our work, all of our actions. We are being watched but not judged. The Earth puts a bit of a face on Stones to make this connection with our human brains. Some call it *anthropomorphic*. My friends and I know it is spiritual.

"We love listening to Earth Mother. She is guiding us now with your MRSA bug. And Jules, I have saved the best for last: The Mayo Clinic is sending a new antibiotic for us to try! Sorry, I've got to leave. We were enjoying ourselves, weren't we?"

Robin left the Stone with Jules and she began to cry. "This must be another one of those releases," Jules thought. "I am not feeling sorry for myself; this is real trauma." Her dad, Jordi, helped her understand this. There was no shortage of conversation through the years to draw from. Jordi took his personal training seriously, often co-leading the local men's group. Mind-Body-Spirit-Emotion. These are the four pillars of a complete human.

"We practice holistic healing around here," Jordi reminded her. "If you've noticed, I pioneered that gig seven years ago, now look at me." It was true. He had a hockey accident that left him lots more seriously injured than he admitted. When a different kind of infection threatened him, he and Robin gathered up Sam and Jules and drove straight to Seattle where there were integrative medical experts who used a broad spectrum for healing.

Even though Robin was the head of Rehabilitative Therapy at Bonner General, they learned a lot in Seattle about rehabilitation and how to help others. As he dropped a kiss onto her forehead, he whispered one word. "Patience"

Jordi visited his daughter often. He loved waking her with a kiss on her forehead and she always felt better after only a few minutes. He had brought his own gift to their conversations by inviting her curiosity. He told her, "This is one of the components of resilience, Little Lady." Jules liked the nicknames her Dad had given her over the years. Little Lady was the newest one; it made her feel grown up.

"What should I be curious about?" she asked.

Her father pulled a face and answered in sing-song, "*Absolutely everything/ Just don't miss anything.* Let's start with gratitude."

Jules was puzzled. "How do gratitude and curiosity connect?"

"Good question. They don't have a precise connection. Instead, they are both components of resilience. To get through your current challenge, we each need to connect with our inner energies. Mine are different than yours—Mom's energies are different, too. In order to heal from this challenge, we all need to identify our own energies and work with them. It's not easy being you right now, but it's no easier watching you."

"I guess I've been pretty well consumed with solving our climate chaos and building community. Until this week, I hadn't even thought of the root of my problem. It's spiritual isn't it?"

Picking up the thread, Jordi said, "The coming years will be filled with climate chaos. Your work as a Drawdown Scholar has turned me on to a couple of great books; I'll try to get up to speed. We all need to become conversant about resilience and self-reliance. Jules, your immediate challenge is to stretch yourself right here, to thrive, from this moment." He emphasized, "Be curious about thriving. That's your goal. I'm here to help."

"Practical stuff," she said out loud. She wondered if she would show him her poem. "You have just given me the end goal. Thanks Dad!" She accepted another kiss on top of her head. Jordi had to leave. He explained he was on a mission to the fire department to pick up the undelivered toys and take them to a storage unit for kids who have a hospital stay longer than a few hours.

He left her with a sticky note: *Components of Resilience—Grit, Life Purpose, Gratitude, Curiosity, and Strength through Adversity, your new secret sauce.* She entered the components of resilience into her digital journal.

Jules laid back on her pillow and closed her eyes. She and Gran had talked about Grit, the Root was connected to her Life Purpose, somehow. Resilience would become part of her plan.

She was grateful to have enough time for a little meditation. Instead, her teammates woke her up with texts: There were Grandmothers who wanted to come! She replied with a smiley face. When?

Chapter 9

ADVANCED GROUP-THINK POWER

As she woke up out of a deep dream, Jules saw that colorful scarves lay in a circle across her legs creating a center piece. How had they sneaked into the room without her hearing them? She reached for a glass of water.

After hellos and hugs, Sara, Dot, Alex and Gail stood up and held hands. Gail flicked on her little electric candle. Jules started with breath and a round of gratitude, describing this as her favorite way to begin their meetings. The Project teammates summarized their research, some with a single sentence, and placed their sticky notes in the middle of the circle.

Jules went first. "Seventeen. This must be our magic number, same as our age. I found 17 Drawdown Solutions for sure already working, or as Gail says, *should be* working in our bioregion."

Alex went next. "Our bioregion has 56,675 very smart people, more than half are farmers or gardeners."

Sara held her sticky note high over her head and twirled. "The mayors have met because Dad insisted, and now they are planning a two-county council meeting in three weeks, just before spring break. We're invited to present!"

Dot didn't mind being last. "The Kootenai Bioregion has 45 abandoned farms with absentee owners and that means we might be able to coax a donation or use eminent domain to acquire those 1200 acres for land use: jobs, housing, regenerative farming, and community collaboration for tree planting. The Land Trust has 20,000 acres more for possible Nature Connection and healing."

Robin came in the front door, quickly crossing the room to Jules' IV drip. In a loud whisper everyone could hear, she said to Jules, "I've brought you that gift from the Mayo Clinic I told you about; it just arrived. There are MRSA patients all over the country and the Mayo Clinic's researchers formed a special task force to distribute this new super-antibiotic. Cross your fingers Jules. We're going to save that leg, right?"

There was, the dreaded words had been spoken. The girls all went silent; Gail watched the blood drain from their faces. Alex took charge. "If you have a battle on your hands, why not call on all of us to form a prayer chain for you? For the past two weeks, while you were here suffering in bed, I've been adding to our inventory lists and knocking on doors. Do you know how many churches there are in Sandpoint? I do! and I will ask for a prayer chain for you all over town."

Before Jules could protest, Dot jumped right in. "Ya, in these two weeks running solo, we've all done big things we didn't know we could do. It's your turn, Jules. I heard you say, 'Zorro to the rescue.' You didn't know you could heal from this nasty superbug, but you can."

Gail chimed in. "You absolutely can heal this. Decide in your mind that you can. Send that news to your heart. Reach out to all of us and our resources. Adversity makes us stronger."

Jules gave a twinkle-eye around the circle. "Yes! I've got this. Thanks for your help; I needed it."

Gail watched the energy build and met Robin's eyes. Something wonderful was happening to these young women. Suddenly they loved giving speeches! Their passion meters were way off the charts.

She said for Robin's benefit, "I've been in bed with a cold and while I stayed away, this brilliant team turned into a power center! Let's have a good practice session. Dazzle me. I want to turn on my camera, is that OK?"

Robin kissed the top of Jules head, gave a finger wave and left the house.

Sara pulled out straws and said, "Long goes first." Everyone took one, including Gail. They joked this was the last thing straws should be used for before they were completely banned from the Earth. "Great, you all left me with No. 1." Sara laughed as everyone handed over their numbers. "Dot is 2, Alex 3, Jules is 4. Gail, you drew No. 5."

Sara prepared to go first. She spread herself out on the floor and pulled things out of her bag. Thirty seconds later, she stood up completely composed. She pointed to Gail's phone on a tripod. "Roll 'em! My topic is Climate Justice: Part of every single subject, all at once, so it's hard to be narrow and specific.

"Justice brings me to local governments. I've been learning those inner workings and what this means. Mind you, my efforts are all bi-partisan—you know me with equality—but that is not what I discovered inside the departments. Adults are not thinking outside the box; they will be ashamed when teenagers expose their narrow thinking."

"Don't forget about diplomacy," Alex shouted out.

Sara continued. "Equality, I am not seeing it. So, Climate Justice begins with all that divides and must create space where the players can talk to one another. Talk is the ingredient missing in politics and government. The mayors of Sandpoint, Sagle, Clark Fork, Hope, Ponderay, Dover, Priest River, and Bonners Ferry have all met and will deliver their first reports to their city councils. Eight mayors! Before the fire season began two years ago, fire prevention was the only other time such a large convergence occurred. OK.

"I need some water." Sara pivoted and leaned over her bag. "Now for the really good news. The mayors agreed on a date when we could come and show the *Introduction to Drawdown*, if that's what we want to do." Cheers erupted.

Gail jumped out of her chair to give Sara a big hug. "Such persuasive power you've got!" she said.

Sara continued without missing a beat. "So, in March, after our team delivers the subject of Drawdown, there must be time allowed for discussion. Who is the best facilitator?"

Gail nodded her head. "I know several; let me ask around."

Sara concluded her report. "Mark your calendars, March 21. Clear away any appointments you have before finals' week. As of now, two weeks before spring break, we are scheduled to present before an audience of our local government at the Sandpoint Auditorium.

Dot jumped right out of her chair and turned the video toward herself. "I will take it from here. You deserve big cheers and more, Sara. March 21 is my 17th birthday and I am going to make it count for something." She looked right into the camera, something Sara had not done. "This is good practice—each one of us can do videos like selfies, which will improve our performance." She laughed, "There's nothing more narcissistic than watching yourself give a speech just before bed.

"A-hem." She cleared her throat. "My broad area is Regeneration. I spent free time for three days going over county records. One of the county clerks, Laura Parsons, is super helpful and has become my Land Use mentor; we have a mutual passion. I will invite her to the big meet-up. We need to give that meeting a jazzy name. How about Convergence? And, we need to snag an interview with the Reader.

"Anyway, Laura Parsons and her assistant, Lori Wells and I found 1200 acres for Regeneration that can be put into a permaculture planning process right away. Regenerating 45 parcels of land will employ a lot of people. After a couple of years of growing food, and people buying fresh food locally, our bioregion can become more self-reliant. I think that is our main goal.

"Talking to Lori and my parents, I realized we forgot to put fundraising anywhere. I need to do a local money map and see where it's flowing now. Argh, I'm in over my head!

"Land Use is really a huge subject. We need to become more involved with tree planting, which could provide summer jobs. Let's look at funding for that as well as the nursery stocks. I think Diane Green and her husband Thom from Greentree Naturals have a few answers. Permission to make them Consultants?"

Dot was on a roll. "There is another Consultant, Jane Fritz. Indigenous Peoples Land Management may be the most interesting Solution on my list. Jane has connections to the three tribes whose land we live on and use. See how delicate this subject might become—in what good way could we ask them how to support the land? Maybe straight on. I will reach out to Jane to hear her recordings of the Nez Perce, Kalispell, and Kootenai tribes first. Did you read about the awful news about Australia burning has included stories of 50,000 years of Aboriginal knowledge—there and everywhere, First People used fire to their benefit."

Jules was amazed. "All I had to do was sit still and look at all that's happening on our Project! Put me down for fund-raising: I love asking people for money."

"Superstars!" Alex exclaimed. "Look what happens when we get turned on. Where did I find the time? Before our Drawdown Scholars Project, I wasted a ton of time on Facebook, Instagram, and who knows what else. Growing up is complicated right?"

Looking into the camera, Alex began her presentation. "We live in a pretty amazing bioregion, alright. I wanted to begin way up at the Canadian border. When I rode up there with my dad a week ago, I learned about a couple of folks who regularly gather people for political fundraising. They call themselves Progressives and we could talk to them to get their ideas. Politics was not exactly one of my categories, but they are well-established and organized. What I like to imagine is people gathered to talk about important local issues.

"I rode with Dad through two load-days. He doesn't know how many loggers there are, but maybe the county would tell us how many logging trucks are registered in both counties. That was Dad's idea. He would like to be retrained to manage a GrowingSpace. He's been inside those 55-ft. geodesic domes over in Clark Fork and has been dreaming about them for growing food on the backside of the calendar. Jules said Gail used to talk about growing food all year when she had her dome. He thinks he's too physically worn out to do much farming, but he's interested in retraining loggers. Isn't that amazing?

"Our trees are even more precious than we believed—who would know better than a logger, right? Dad is ready to leave his job. He says he can see the harm being done to the forests in our bioregion. He loves this word, bioregion. Turns out my dear old dad has become a contemplative man, driving his logging truck alone all those years.

"We took a drive together in the car and talked about the forests up Lightning Creek in Clark Fork and all around the lake. This is a big place—3,192 square miles. Everything we can do to protect this bioregion will contribute to Drawdown. Protection is the key word and maybe my life's work, huh?

"I also counted the non-profits; more about that next time. I want to discover each of their connections to climate." Alex bowed to the camera signaling she was done.

"Wahoo!" Gail stood up and turned off the video. "Marvelous work, all of you! Past halfway, we need a break. Jules has a grand presentation too. Take ten." She handed her phone to Jules. "Will you label this recording and send it to all of us, please?"

Gail took up Jules' water pitcher. "Be right back." Samantha came in to change the pee bag and check on Jules. "Are you hanging in, Sis?"

Jules' eyes popped open. "I have a miracle coming any minute. Mom plugged in the new medicine from Mayo Clinic. Did you hear? We're scheduled to present to local city governments before spring break."

"No. Wow! Awesome." Sam rolled Jules over on her side and rubbed her back. Then she went around the bed and rolled her the other way. All kinds of moans and groans.

"I need a bit of a break, too." Sam told her. "I'm writing my college application essay; it's tough going right now. Listen. I formed a neat network of women from my fundraising project last year. You could do a presentation for them, if you want."

"Cool. You and I need to talk to Dot. She wants to map the flow of money through the bioregion. So many great ideas, and I really want to hear more about your project, ok?"

"You were there Jules!" They rolled their eyes at one another, as if to say, "Duh," but without words and trying to be a bit nicer to one another. The sisters had discovered the difference between being there and being ALL there, present and attentive. Mindfulness was something their family talked about at mealtimes together.

Gail arrived quietly with a fresh pitcher of ice water and pivoted to sit with her notebook. She drew furiously—being a visual learner has its upside, but not everyone sees the same things. There were many key words in the concept of bioregion, why hadn't she thought of fundraising? Maybe it would solve itself. Usually that's not the case with other people's money.

Jules called the meeting back and asked Gail to turn on the video. She had rehydrated and felt better after her rubdown and her sister-talk. This was all she needed to launch into her turn.

"I just learned this really cool thing about our new year: Symbolically, 2020 means clear vision. There is so much energy swirling to support our Project. As it turns out many Solutions have been active throughout our bioregion for 100 years, even as our ecosystems have been damaged, sometimes severely degraded. In the same ten minutes it takes to acknowledge the beauty of this place, we can decide to protect what we have and restore what has been harmed.

"The 17 Solutions on the list must be shared for collaboration to happen. When we finish talking and planning, we will start to work as a community. I'm thinking about this word—*exaggerate*. I'm not sure of if that is the exact right word. Visualize the Solutions here at the present time registering on a scale at 1 or 2. Once exaggerated, or energized, or worked, each Solution scales up to 10."

She passed around her list. Gail was impressed. "Educating Girls is on the rise in our bioregion!" She couldn't help clapping her hands in delight. "Sorry to interrupt."

Jules continued. "Sam reminded me that fundraising was her team's topic and they raised $9,300 by showing their project to groups outside of school. We need to cross-pollinate with last year's Project participants. Okay, fundraising sits in the bigger picture. Over and over, I choose Solutions. In my presentation, the first slide is all 100 Solutions listed by Sectors.

PACHAMAMA ALLIANCE
Drawdown Solutions by Sector

Land Use
Tropical Forests
Temperate Forests
Peatlands
Afforestation
Bamboo
Forest Protection
Indigenous Peoples' Land
  Management
Perennial Biomass
Coastal Wetlands

Energy
Wind Turbines (Onshore)
Solar Farms
Rooftop Solar
Geothermal
Nuclear
Wind Turbines (Offshore)
Concentrated Solar
Wave and Tidal
Methane Digesters (Large)
Biomass
Solar Water
In-Stream Hydro
Cogeneration
Methane Digesters (Small)
Waste-to-Energy
Micro Wind
Energy Storage (Distributed)
Energy Storage (Utilities)
Grid Flexibility
Microgrids

Food
Reduced Food Waste
Plant-Rich Diet
Silvopasture
Regenerative Agriculture
Tropical Staple Trees
Conservation Agriculture
Tree Intercropping
Managed Grazing
Clean Cookstoves
Farmland Restoration
Improved Rice
  Cultivation
Multistrata Agroforestry
System of Rice
  Intensification
Composting
Nutrient Management
Farmland Irrigation
Biochar

Transport
Electric Vehicles
Ships
Mass Transit
Trucks
Airplanes
Cars
Telepresence
High-speed Rail
Electric Bikes
Trains
Ridesharing

Materials
Refrigerant Management
Alternative Cement
Water Saving - Home
Bioplastic
Household Recycling
Industrial Recycling
Recycled Paper

Women and Girls
Educating Girls
Family Planning
Women Smallholders

Building and Cities
District Heating
Insulation
LED Lighting (Household)
Heat Pumps
LED Lighting (Commercial)
Building Automation
Walkable Cities
Smart Thermostats
Landfill Methane
Bike Infrastructure
Smart Glass
Water Distribution
Green Roofs
Net Zero Buildings
Retrofitting

DRAWDOWN SCHOLARS & ENTREPRENEURS

Spirit of Change
FOOD Sector: 8 Solutions
- Composting
- Reduced Food Waste
- Plant Rich Diet
- Regenerative Agriculture
- Farmland Restoration
- Silvopasture
- Multistrata Agraforestry
- Biochar

Regeneration
LAND USE: 4 Solutions
- Regenerative Agriculture
- Indigenous Peoples Land Management
- Aforestation
- Forest Protection

Bioregion-Boundary & Bonner Counties
WOMEN & GIRLS: 2 Solutions
- Women Smallholders
- Educating Girls

Climate Justice
MIXED SECTORS: 3 Solutions
- Rooftop Solar
- Bioplastic
- Alternative Cement

Across the top of her drawing she had written in block letters, DRAW-DOWN SCHOLARS & ENTREPRENEURS. "With the great research of my Project teammates, I created this new handout; it will look better on PowerPoint."

She continued, "I'm the central collector of Solutions that are almost working in our bioregion. When we looked through the list of 100 Drawdown Solutions, we found many small efforts here in our bioregion. One of my tasks is to create a seamless connection to the extensive work a decade ago by a group here in Sandpoint called Climate CAN. Gail was a member of that group and gave me two names to call: Nancy Gilliam, Model Forest Policy Program at *MFPP.org* and Jean Gerth, *350Sandpoint.org*. We are lucky to have these savvy allies nearby."

"I could do introductions," Gail offered. "We might have more Solutions if we coordinate with good people like this. Remember, more is not necessarily better."

Jules agreed. "I would love introductions! From the top—Alex has the First Sector, Women and Girls. We will focus on the most powerful Solutions in this Sector. Women and Girls need to be included in every action and every decision. For Women Smallholders, we can develop a small loan program. Fundraising could crossover here and we will become a bank for other entrepreneurs. That's one of Alex's big topics.

"Sara has picked up where the Climate Action Network laid good groundwork for us in the local government. This began a decade ago. Back then, the game changers took up retrofitting city and county buildings for lighting, insulation and energy efficiency. We didn't know they would be Solutions! When those efforts were folded into Nancy's non-profit, *MFPP.org*, she scaled up those efforts to the county level and focused on the Comprehensive Plan. That's huge work. Nancy has raised enough funds to form a national network of 44 counties fluent in climate adaptation and mitigation.

"Sara has parlayed a great advantage by expanding the conversations her dad has with the Mayor during their 30-mile bike rides and workouts at the Y. Her Sector is Materials which crosses into a Sector we will spend more time on later—Buildings & Cities. She and Jon talked to Waste Management and proposed a food waste recycling project similar to what Boise has done. Sara suggested our two counties distribute a starter supply of bioplastic bags for everyone's kitchen, opening the door for city-wide composting of food wastes. Yay! If bioplastics are used in every household, food scraps become compost rather than methane at the transfer stations. Food waste becomes valuable soil amendments, as long as the compost gets hot enough."

Jules was on a roll. "On plastic, our bioregion has a problem like everywhere else in the world. The looming question is—what can we do with it? Can it be a resource for something?" She held her index finger over her lips for dramatic effect. "Shhhh. I received leaked information that is headline news! One of the boys' teams is working the plastic angle for us. They propose the three north counties recycle our plastic as a durable material resource and make things out of it: Decking materials and outdoor benches top their list. Their motto is, *If Trex can do it, the Panhandle can too.*"

She scooched back against her pillows to sit up straighter. "All good. Stay tuned for more." Jules flashed Sara a twinkle-eye. "My sector is Food and we're lucky that so many Solutions have been working in this area for so long. Forming a cooperative new partnership between gardeners and farmers will be fun.

"All the playful meetings the gardeners have could spill over to all the serious meetings the ranchers and farmers have. Each of them just needs representatives in the others' meetings. These two diverse groups need to cross pollinate: I propose one big celebration during the Fair and maybe a monthly meeting at the Co-op. Everyone goes there and it's pretty neutral territory.

"Focus on Regeneration: This is a Solution as well as Dot's Land Use assignment. Because we live in the Pacific Northwest, we don't want to lose our climate; it makes things green—our growing season is long enough for winter squash, growing brilliantly colorful before it snows. We're promoting all the ways to draw carbon out of the atmosphere. We will ask the new carbon tracker start-up, Nori, and a Drawdown team to come measure for us. Some of the most interesting work will happen with the new jobs—Dot covers this. For the Solution called Plant Rich Diets, we must begin in elementary school and integrate growing a garden into the curriculum. Michele Murphree started a garden at each of the elementary schools. I need to talk to her. She probably won't remember me from Northside, but I remember when she visited our garden.

"Eating well was something my mom talked a lot about when I was in 4th and 5th grades. She calls it behavior modification. Children as young as 6th grade choose to become vegans. That's a wonderful thing because they can teach other kids about eating less meat and dairy.

"No need to talk about plant rich diets among ranchers, they have other Solutions on my list. Gail used to be a rancher. She said she would enjoy talking to them about their contribution to carbon removal. The extension agents will help with silvopasture, integrating trees, forage and managed grazing. Believe it or not, none of this is happening here in the Kootenai Bioregion. Drawdown Scholars are going to be the change makers!"

Everyone nodded and Jules threaded her thoughts. "Major players are the ag-extension agents. Fortunately, Gail did the Master Gardeners' course and the school garden project so she knows some of the players; these relationships only need reviving."

Gail chimed in, "The elders have been inoculated with the Drawdown bug. I had lunch today with two of our gifted and extraordinary elders. Everyone in this room is becoming a weaver through our concentric circles. Let's all begin to quicken our family and friends."

Jules cleared her throat again and received a twinkle-eye from Gail. "I've read a book in my spare time, *Burn: Using Fire to Cool the Earth*, a primer about biochar. I'll never again look at slash piles the same way.

"Alex, if your Women's Smallholder enterprise takes off someday, I hope you will fund me as an entrepreneur. Creating biochar will grow rich connections to the Earth. Biochar is so good for the soils; it will make us wealthy as a people. Our wealth is in our soils where the carbon lives.

"My plan is to make biochar in three states: Idaho, Oregon, and Washington. Our soils will begin to recover to pre-glacial quality, before the glacier retreated and the ice dam burst that held ancient Lake Missoula. You know, that glacial event washed away the soil in all three states. Best guess is that it took half a millennium, but it left us with bedrock or deep sandy soil.

"Biochar as a soil amendment and as incompletely burned wood - carbon – forms a structure like an earth-condo where mycelium can expand. As a perpetual source of carbon as nourishment, it feeds those intricate threads of mycelium forward into the future for 1,000 years. Here is one of our magical connections—Biochar helps Earth regenerate herself." This was a strong ending and Jules knew it.

Alex jumped up, "Bravo!" and turned the phone video towards Gail.

"Rights of Nature is a Level 3 and Level 4 subject," Gail began. "Do you remember seeing Will Grant in the Drawdown introduction teaching the effectiveness scale? He talked about the four levels. Our purpose is discovering how to cause change by scaling up each of our Solutions. We change the game in every Sector, moving from Level 1—personal change; 2—family; 3—schools and other institutions; up to Level 4—policy, to sustain change. Rights of Nature only operates on the scale at Levels 3 and 4. I've got easy examples.

"On skis, I give respect and honor to the mountain while I am floating down the fall line. I close my eyes when I am floating in my kayak, but neither of these affects your actions. Level 2 happens if I tell you a story about my activities and you join me. We could have a candlelight flotilla on a Full Moon night and feel teary-eyed about our precious lake, our precious mountains, the bounty of our huckleberries and morel mushrooms. When we bring the local government into this conversation and ask them to pass a law to grant equal rights to our lake and to our mountain and forests, then deeper protections become possible.

"All the efforts in our fight against that second bridge across Lake Pend Oreille would be rendered irrelevant if we had local laws in place. With a Rights of Nature law, that second bridge across the lake, the smelter on the river, and mining of all kinds become legally impossible. This will be a game changer—it is much easier to talk about than to accomplish, but talk is the initiator of all things.

"With a Rights of Nature bill in place, just like our Constitution's Bill of

Rights for human beings, doing anything to harm our lake becomes illegal. Ecocide is spreading worldwide. Our local government can change environmental policy. They do not need state or federal approval. This is the movement called Rights of Nature.

"Our efforts as Drawdown Scholars will be designed to scale up protections from almost zero now to ten! In our bioregion we have so much to protect. You and I will make a big difference when we stand before our local government officials on Spring Equinox and offer a preview of your hard work. It's like a slow cooker—when I tell them this much about Rights of Nature, they will have to talk among themselves. The process began with you, Drawdown Scholars! Give yourselves a bow."

Gail turned off the recorder. After a few moments of silence, she pointed her index finger to the ceiling and offered a writing tip, "Your serious writing starts next. Clarity will come to you at the intersection where research meets well-constructed sentences. You'll see." She handed out sheets of paper. On one side were the outline steps and on the other side, reference books and rules for citations.

"Take a week to read one of these books, visit these websites. As you gather your information for writing also gather the reference citations. Don't leave a website unless you capture the exact URL address and note the date. Academia is precise. Cruise around, have fun. I will be back in one week, right? Turn up your inner fire a little, we're just a bit behind schedule.

"Next week, we will talk in depth about your papers. You can be thinking about your outline, think of it as a scaffold where you hang the things you have learned. Organize your thoughts into Introduction, Literature Review, Methods, and Conclusion. Twenty pages will come easy."

Just as she ended her instructions, Gail added a prayer: "I give thanks to the trees who originally gave us this 100% recycled paper that we can recycle again. Jules you're doing double duty. When you pull off your miracle, you will discover your true strength for the rest of your life. Become a miracle worker, Jules!"

Gail gathered her papers and notebook, listening to the Scholars groan under the weight of their work ahead. "Through the writing, you will gain acknowledgement for your brilliant work," she encouraged. "The old saying, 'Talk is cheap' washes away with good crisp writing and a bibliography to go with it. You will be surprised how academic writing deepens your knowledge. My ride is here.

"You know me, I love the writing the best. Have a fun week. Gather your outline. Send me emails." Very brief hugs and kisses and the room felt the void.

Chapter 10

TANGO PRACTICE

Jules daily battle with MRSA had begun in earnest with the new antibiotic; it had been a month of touch and go. Her fever broke, her white count was responding, and Robin sent an email update that made everyone hopeful. When Gail arrived with Kenny, she thought they were 30 minutes early, but several others were there ahead of them. The front room from the door all the way through to the kitchen had been transformed. The hospital bed was gone. In its place a low table with an altar—Jules had acquired the Sister Scarves and used them before every meeting to add the quality of ceremony. Candles were already lit creating an aura of enchantment.

Seventeen folding chairs fit comfortably in two rows around the table. Jon had come, beaming at Sara. Dot's mom and dad stopped in for 30 minutes on their way to Costco. Alex's dad had achieved hero status among the girls, and they were excited to meet the lumberjack after everything that they had heard. Jordi and Samantha stood together as Jules announced that her Spokane docs had released her to their family doctor for follow-up; she could begin walking therapy in another week.

Alex rang a little bell and Sara led the welcomes with a three-breath moment of togetherness.

Each of the Drawdown Scholars presented a crisp seven-minute speech about her Sector and Jules masterfully introduced the concept of Solutions. Sara concluded the hour-long gathering. "We have to send you home before the blizzard hits full force," she said. "But we ask you to share your passions, your experience, wherever your experience fits into our efforts. We can't move into the future alone. This is a collaborative effort from now on. Just tell your Scholar and we will all get the message. Hang on for this great joy ride, we're feeling so empowered." She gave Jon and Dex her twinkle-eye, showering her dazzling smile on the whole crowd.

Stepping forward, Gail wiped tears from her eyes and applauded the four Drawdown Scholars. "An especially warm welcome to any of you family members who wish to come to the luncheon we are having as a fundraiser and practice presentation for these young women. We need you and your friends. We're assembling an elegant Circle of Consultants, so please join us. Our first meeting will be a casual lunch at the Tango Café. Each one of you, dear relations, are welcome and encouraged to join our Circle. We will gather next Friday, February 14—Valentine's Day offers a sweet backdrop for teens, families, friends and elders who want to work for the Earth."

Gail pivoted to Jules. "You're going back to school on Monday. Congratulations! You turned the corner quickly. While you students continue with your protests, *#FridaysforFuture,* I invite everyone to join us at the Tango Café. Allow these awesome relations and powerful women to celebrate your work. After our meeting at the Tango, we will all walk over to Farmin Park together for your afternoon sit-in. I'll see you next week."

Gran, a horsewoman all her life with a strong slender body to prove it, stepped back and said, "Great. Count on me for lunch Gail. You Scholars are doing brilliant work. Bravo." Gran threw on her poncho, wrapped her hair up under her cowgirl's hat, and with keys jingling grabbed her bag. In a flurry, she smooched Jules and whispered, "I love you" then slipped out the door.

Gran met Robin on the sidewalk. They talked for a minute, then Robin opened the door, stepping into the chaos that Gran had created. Most of the guests were gathering their things to leave. The girls had presented a much briefer practice session with their invited guests, each of them giving what Gail called 'an elevator-speech version,' keeping it short and sweet. The practice of brevity was good for everyone.

Word about the Drawdown Scholars was spreading fast. People were already talking about the team. With high-fives all around everyone dispersed. Kenny stood with Gail, his arm around her shoulder, absorbing all the good vibes.

Inside the downtown Sandpoint bank building awaits a surprise—a two-story water feature, more than a mere fountain, creates a serene display of life in the foyer. Many books were written and kicked off here. Gail felt a special love for the place, its convenience, and the inner peace the cascading water provided.

Stepping up to the counter of the Tango Café to place an order, another surprise awaits: Wholesome food, not too fast, but always delicious. A special event was happening here today that the teen science team had arranged. Could they run a tab for the group?

Touching her heart in a gesture of love, Gail began the meeting. "Each one of you made special arrangements, scheduling this as your errand day around town. The Drawdown Scholars thank you for your efforts. We are half-way through our semester and accelerated learning has created a remarkable bloom in these young women." She held the book, *Drawdown: The Most Comprehensive Plan Ever Proposed to Reverse Global Warming*, over her head so the Circle, including twelve new faces, could see clearly. She read the title, loud and clear and said, "This is what all the fuss is about."

Gail handed the mic to Sara. "I can't wait to talk with each of you; let's make that happen this afternoon. Drawdown is the only plan for reversing global warming. This book has changed all of us, from fearful during our climate protests at Farmin, to empowered women. First thing we did as a group was to show the *Introduction to Drawdown* movie to the middle school AP science group and discovered, we have the goods here." She fanned out the book in front of her. "We now have agency over our fear of climate change. We know what to do and every day our task gets bigger—that's half the fun.

"I have found real Solutions, but my overall focus is Climate Justice. Why? Because we live in one of the most peaceful, underrated places on Earth. Climate migrants and refugees are going to discover us, and we want to be ready with the welcome wagon." Sara knew those were high energy words. This concept of receiving people from all directions was not new to Sandpoint. "We will be ready with housing, jobs, and a supply chain to keep folks in the Solutions rather than creating new problems.

"I want to acknowledge two Consultants who paved the way for our work. I am so excited they are here with us today. Nancy Gilliam is the Director for the Model Forestry Policy Program *MFPP.org* a national non-profit located up Sagle Road. She spearheaded the Climate Action Network more than a decade ago. And Jean Gerth is here; she leads *350Sandpoint*. Being best friends, they are a powerful team keeping the subject of climate change alive for us. Thank you both."

She gave a twinkle eye to Alex and handed her the mic. "Hi." She began to laugh-cry. "Thank you for joining our team. We need every single one of you. Today in your honor we have set up a tipi donated by Tipi-Lady, Debra Williams. We've been rather cold at Farmin Park, now we can all be a bit warmer on Friday afternoons. We hope to attract more attention." She pulled out a red handkerchief and blew her nose.

"You can see the scale of our project when you visualize the boundaries of our two counties. We are the Kootenai Bioregion. Gail likes to call the Panhandle 'Idaho chimney.' Our bioregion includes ten townships, 56,675 people (est. 2018 census) and 3,192 square miles. My task has been to compile a complete inventory of everything here, the people..." pausing, she flashed one of her most radiant smiles and added, "each of you appear on my list of assets. I have begun an inventory of trees, every variety. Sprouts and Bob Wilson helped me. Jennifer and Kate are here, our wonderful extension agents, have responded to all my questions. I need all of you.

"Many around this table are here because of this inventory. Gail knows amazing women. Besides the overview of our bioregion, my focus on Solutions is an entire Sector called Women and Girls. All you need to hear right now is that our power is on the rise."

She handed the mic to Dot. "This has been said before—we need you. You women are the brain-trust of our two counties. Organizing for better use of our Lands, that's my Sector. There are lots of positive actions waiting to scale up the Land Use Sector. As Gail says, we need to 'harvest the wisdom' of your experience. That'll make our job as the younger generation so much easier.

"The bridge we are creating right here between young and old, between ranchers and farmers—talking to each other, this is the whole enchilada." Dot smiled at her food metaphor and paused after her punchline, because that was served for lunch today. "Together we will create a model for all of rural America."

She handed the mic to Jules who had wheeled her chair back from the table and with Gail's help, stood up. Everyone seemed as surprised as her grandmother who leaped to her feet and said with a twinkle in her eye, "Can I always hold your hand?" Her words were meant for everyone in the room.

"You're looking at a miracle," Jules said. "The doc told me I could begin by standing for ten minutes at a time, so I thought I would practice here. My overview is Solutions. We found more than 20 of these 100 Solutions visible in our bioregion already. Our focus with this Junior Project is to let everyone see how much opportunity we have at our fingertips. If we all see what is working—sometimes at an efficiency rate of 2 or 3 on a scale of 10—and bump that up to 9 or 10 then spread the word, well, we can expect headlines across the country. Thanks also to both of you Reader reporters for accepting our invitation. Local news strengthens our communities."

Gail had invited reporters from the Sandpoint Reader and the Bee to be present and become Consultants, if they chose. They were scribbling notes as fast as they could write, even though Gail and the team had provided them with a Press Release before the luncheon.

Jules continued, finding her voice through a story: "Ever since I was in the 2nd grade at the Northside School when Gail started our Garden Club, I have loved gardening. Growing food has been such a passion that I apprenticed to Diane Green last year." She dazzled her mentor with a twinkle eye and mouthed "Thank you" as she extended her hands toward Diane.

"Look around these tables—more than half of you have something to do with growing food. That's how important this Food Sector is for our bioregion. Through photosynthesis, from early spring through autumn every year, Mother Earth regenerates through leaf and stem, sending sugars to her roots for storage. Most of that regeneration is carbon storage. I created this list to simplify things for you." Gail circled the tables handing out the list.

"We are so happy to share our 17 Solutions with all of you. We want you to know that eight mayors have called an area-wide council meeting, only the second one ever. Our team will present a PowerPoint to our collective local government on March 21. Please come if you can. We need your support."

Jules tried to be graceful getting back into her wheelchair. Gail read Jules' report and knew what her last line would be—she signaled to Gran to help. "All hands on deck! As Paul Hawken, Drawdown's first mentor, always says— Game on!"

Gail took the mic and said, "Those action words belong to the instigator of Drawdown and editor of the book. The brilliance of Paul Hawken's work accelerated when he gathered his scholars together. Most of them worked for two or three years to bring us this book. What we have discovered in the last month is his one great truth: Knowing which Solutions are locally present offers an opportunity to see and increase their cascade of benefits. These Solutions are so valuable we will want to scale up anyway. And, we will draw the carbon down from the atmosphere, lessening the greenhouse effect and taming climate chaos. Ten years and done.

"I will field questions and indicate which one of our Drawdown Scholars has the answer."

Diane raised her hand first, "Wow! Thanks for this good start. I want to suggest that once a month area gardeners and farmer-ranchers 'meet-up' at the Co-op, maybe across the street under the trees. Many of us do our errands in town on Wednesday because the Farmers Market happens. How about starting the last Wednesday in May? That will give everyone time to adjust. If it's still chilly, I could bring my propane high tunnel heater."

Everyone began to clap then Gran raised her hand. "I think I can help gather the ranchers. I will work on them. We are a stubborn lot, you know."

Maria stood up. "I am really passionate about food waste. I would like to gather together a group of restaurant owners whom I know personally—Dex can probably help me. We need to tackle this whole subject of food waste. Boise has a good model for composting food waste, but there is another angle: Perfectly good food is being tossed out that could go to the senior centers, to the elder housing centers, and to the soup kitchens. There is a built-in stream of donated food from the Farmers Market already going to the Food Bank, but I know Tango Café tosses plenty of perfectly good food that could stream to Ellen at the Senior Center. Since you live in Bonners Ferry, Gail will you help me?"

Gail was happy to be called on for help and felt teary-eyed. "Jules has the Food Sector and is grateful for our help. You know, I've only been here part-time." She sent her long-time yoga teacher and swami a twinkle-eye smile. "That is changing."

Gail's special friend from Spokane stood up next. "From reading energy, I am the odd woman in this group, I'm from Spokane. But I have lived a long time on the edge of the city and in Deer Park. I am taking this beautiful story back to my granddaughters and their friends. We are overdue for these action steps." She put her hands together and bowed to Gail and the Scholars.

Before handing the mic to Alex, Gail explained that her friend from Spokane, also named Gail, was an artist who developed epic Earth Art; she offered original illustrations for the Scholar's PowerPoint in one month. Alex took the mic and uttered a joyous expletive, "Fuck," then turned beet red. "Sorry to be so rude," she apologized. "I am overwhelmed and that's my favorite word to let go of pressure." Regaining her composure, she asked in slow-mo, "Did you say one month? OK. Who has anything to add to our inventory?"

Marilyn's hand shot up. She was there because the winter rains had already melted the high-country snow. "I want to mention Ecosystem Evolution. At the Native Plant Society, we have restoration specialists who focus on all layers of ecosystems, from mycelium to ground covers, to small and large plants, working up to the short trees and finally to the tall trees. If you just plant a tree, you leave out all of these important support systems."

Alex gave Marilyn a hug. "Now I know why you're in this Consultant's Circle. Thank you so much for your wisdom. Where have you been hiding?"

Marilyn laughed and in her gravelly voice answered, "Long story."

Diane explained. "For 38 years, Marilyn has lived all the way up Grouse Creek. You should visit sometime."

"Dad and I have been to the top of Strawberry Mountain," Alex replied. "Is that your drainage?"

Marilyn nodded and offered her biggest smile. "We'll talk in the tipi."

Finally, Perky stood up and reached for the mic. "These girls make me so proud. So proud! I have watched you blossom before my eyes. The challenges that Gail presented you with might be unique in our school system, but the important thing I see is how you each have stepped up to the task. I suggest you make a handbook from your efforts—a resource manual for the other 42 Idaho counties. Diane can help. Jennifer can help. We can all help! Let's make this a bioregion challenge to the school districts, like a quest, find your regional solutions.

"Every bioregion in Idaho needs to be identified, probably through our county extension offices. Let us help you spread the word and grow your efforts beyond the Panhandle. Please, call on me to read your work when you get closer to the end. I would feel honored. Thank you."

As principal of the rural elementary school, Perky only had Jules as a student. But as AP science teacher for the district, she got to know these young Scholars through her special credit middle school courses. Perky attended their *Introduction to Drawdown* preview at the middle school, but until now had not followed up. Another piece of the puzzle fell into place.

Sara took the mic. "Who would like a piece of carrot cake before we walk over to Farmin Park? I know I would." She raised her hand. "It's the house specialty." She grinned. Jon had told Sara that organizers always find ways to keep their audience longer. She was ready. After counting ten hands for cake and carrying the mic with her to the counter to place the order, she continued. "Let's look at the list of local Solutions. Do any surprise you? Dot will write down your answers."

Sara called on Loie after she looked at her name tag. "Only a few of us have seen the *Introduction to Drawdown* movie," Loie said. "I would like to suggest that. For me, the surprise on this list is biochar." Several women lowered their hands and nodded.

Ellen's hand was still raised. "I'm surprised to see Family Planning is not on the list but Alternative Cement is." She smiled broadly—Ellen was someone who could get both sides talking. She had grown her effectiveness in her elder years as director of the Senior Center and had her finger on the pulse of all issues effecting seniors. Everyone was glad to see a natural politician at the table.

Nancy Gilliam hadn't said much until Sara called on her. "How are we doing, Nancy?"

"My hand is not raised, but I am astounded, pleasantly surprised by your work," Nancy said. "You make our job at *MFPP.org* so much easier. I love seeing a few of our efforts from ten years ago. The items listed here that we approached include Rooftop Solar, LED lighting, and Smart Thermostats. We encouraged retrofitting for insulation and triple-pane windows. A couple of our government buildings have reached Platinum status."

She leaned down to Alex and whispered conspiratorially. "I say fuck twenty times a day." She addressed the whole group. "I am here to help you with the Forest Solutions. I have worked through county comprehensive plans for resilient communities in 40 different U.S. locations. I will help you with outreach when you get your rural manual put together. We need that. I will see you in the tipi every Friday."

Cake was served and everyone with a sweet tooth smiled. Gail pulled a ball cap out of her bag and dropped in $20. "I'm passing the hat for food and contributions. These girls will need recycled paper and soy ink. The teens in the tipi probably need dried fruit and nuts to snack on. Pitch-in only if it's easy for you."

"Never doubt that a small group of thoughtful, committed citizens can change the world; for, indeed, that's all who ever have."

~**Margaret Mead**

Chapter 11

IN THE FARMIN TIPI

#FRIDAYSFORFUTURE

Eighteen teenagers sat in circle around a little propane heater. As was tradition, everyone took a bit of sage smudge before entering, leaving any negative energy at the door. Then they squeezed in together.

Like Gail's old tipi, also made by Tipi-Lady, this was the largest size at 24 ft. in diameter. There were elegant paintings on the liner, mostly Native-inspired symbols, and wild animal designs decorated the interior. It felt nice and toasty inside when Gail and Gran rolled Jules over the threshold. Half of the Consultants from Tango Café were able to come.

Samantha was the organizer for the Friday events, and she welcomed each person, most of whom she knew from somewhere besides school. She squealed welcomes to her personal friends, Nancy and Loie. Sam introduced them together, remembering how she'd worked the tree loads when All Seasons Garden Center received shipments of bare rooted stock. That was when Nancy called on Loie to supervise. Those were good days when young and old worked together.

Speaking up, Loie said, "Thank you for this glorious welcoming energy. Teens and elders—like the old-old days. Have you invited your grandparents?" Loie clearly was the oldest one present.

One of the regulars, Jason said, "No, I haven't. Do you think they would come?"

Nancy answered him. "This is no time to be shy. It's 2020 and time for clear vision. Why not ask?"

As the older women found camp chairs emptied for them, they accepted and settled in. Ellen had been in this Circle of teens many times and she huddled together with them. "Sorry, I can't stay, but I had to come and say hello. Remember, my office door is always open to you."

When Linda Navarre ducked her head through the opening, cheers erupted. Every student loved her 7th grade art classes before the arts were replaced by technology and engineering design. Coming close behind, Perky whispered to Linda, "Seems like we should add art back in, just to keep kids interested in learning."

Overhearing the whispers, Masai sat straighter in the chair she had been offered. "Art needs to be added back in for its therapeutic goodness."

Everyone recognized another boy, Trent, for the murals he created around town. "We usually speak up in here so everyone can hear us," he said. "I like what I'm hearing. Maybe we could invite Linda and Masai to bring us therapeutic art on Fridays?"

Maria came in just in time to hear that. "I would come for therapeutic art too. How can I help?"

As the last one smudged, Maria closed the door flap. Samantha tied up her long hair in a messy ponytail and began drumming—other kids picked up their drums. Within five minutes everyone was gathered into the same space and harmonized their energies. Sam ended the drumming with three extra loud bangs on her drum. "A warm welcome to our visitors. We are here to talk about all kinds of things: the headlines, other protestors, the weather, stuff. Not that we don't love making a fuss over you, we do, but we would love it if you would become regulars."

After her sweet little speech, Sara grinned from ear to ear. "Hey dudes, we have just had lunch with these amazing elders and now we step into the energy of therapeutic art. What can we make? There is such a feeling of brokenness inside of our grief about the Earth."

Maria sat on the ground next to Ann Masai, but she had a big voice. "First of all, it is healthy to feel grief, I mean really feel it. I will come next Friday and offer an Art of Grief process, if you would like that." Yeah! sounded all around the circle. Maria, turned to Masai and Linda, "Can we pull this off, impromptu?"

Samantha looked at Jules. "Tell us how your meeting went."

"Our AP teacher has an interesting custom of trying to use a cloak of secrecy." Jules explained. "She told us not to talk about our subjects. That might be because they may morph into something other than how they appeared at the beginning. It's true; we didn't know all about our subject until we crossed our 30-day line."

Looking at the elders in her audience, Jules continued. "We are the first generation to be raised totally digitally. With the ability to talk to the other side of the world easily, we hear about tragic news as soon as it happens. We have become numb to death, but we have not become numb to Earth's weather being the cause: Greed is the cause.

"We live in a strange time growing beyond Earth's sustainable limits, that's the cause of her changes. Consequences of this overreach make headlines but fail to deal with the root causes. This is different from when you grew up. At least this is what I have learned in the past year in this STEM class when our studies started with the massive WWII Manhattan Project. We have that leftover grief, our own grief, and everyone else's grief, too."

Dot spoke next. "I mean, how weird is it to carry heavy sadness over typhoons in the Philippines? Mom says she could barely find the Philippines on the globe. She said hurricanes have always happened, but they were never headline news. She remembers maybe just one story about Hurricane Andrew from her teen years. She was raising prize heifers and had no interest in climate at all. Sure, schools still closed when it snowed a foot, but that was about it. The constant bombardment of weather destruction is new in our generation!"

Sara waved her arm around the circle, "For this Circle of Consultants—the elders who want to help—I want to lift the cloak of secrecy a little bit. Our team is working on Solutions to global warming. Here in the Kootenai Bioregion, we found so much already working, but those Solutions are not working enough or efficiently or cooperatively. I think cooperation is the key to community."

Linda Navarre spoke next. "One thing you and your parents taught me is that life and power occur in cycles. Earth is going through a cycle of change now—we must feel with her, admire how powerful change is for her. After all, Earth is our Mothership. I knew this when I was your age. We as elders, sitting here with you, can explain cycles of our lives. As Gail has said, we are inside a spiral of development. Perhaps the Earth's people are going through a collective, adolescent, rites-of-passage time. If we help one another process pain and do the things to make our lives more comfortable, the end of this new decade will be better than the end of the last decade. Maybe we will grow up as a species of Sapiens."

Everyone was silent. Gail felt both joy and grief and wiped her tears on her bandana. Her memories with each of the Consultants were thanks to the Earth, and now she inhaled deeply to return, mindfully, to the tipi. She drew another bucket from her well of stubborn optimism. Her heart-joy came from these shining faces and inherent creative possibilities.

Suddenly, they could hear the wind—everyone looked up. Snow was falling across the tipi opening. The deep quiet inside the circle felt holy and full of promise. "Who has a story to send us into dreamland?" Alex asked. One of the activities of *#FridaysforFuture* in Sandpoint involved story-time and maybe a nap.

No one spoke for another minute until Jules broke the silence. "I do. While I was still in that hospital bed last week, I had a visitor. It feels now like she came from another world. She's local to Sandpoint but she works with her ancestral lineage from Nevada. Her name is Karie Lee and she's a shamanic practitioner. She read the energy in me and in the room and knew what I needed. We entered a spiritual trance together and visited the tree where my accident happened. Here is the story of that journey.

"Karie guided me to locate a favorite tree. For me there is only one. Through my childhood I played around that tree and its root, endlessly entertaining myself. With this simple invitation, a part of my spirit went to the root and followed it down into the ground. Below the surface of the Earth there were many roots, some as big around as the tree trunk. I went down-down until I found the heart of my tree. It wasn't hard to find because it was shaped like a big knot underground.

"The root had circled a stone and then kept growing down. When I reached out to touch the stone, I could feel it was the center of the tree's power and the center of its memory system. While I was touching it, a download of weather came across my mind's inner eye. It was amazing that the Stone was so much older than the Tree. Both shared memories, but the Stone's images went back thousands of years.

"Just like Linda said, I was shown how the Earth constantly produces storms: windstorms, fire storms, water events in all seasons. I was amazed when the tree congratulated me for being born! She said I had come into a time of acceleration. Trees and humans both need to find ways to shelter in place, to create tighter communities, to become more cooperative. This is the wisdom of the trees. Do you know, the tree told me, that one of its main nutrients came through her root network from the other side of the ridge. Underground mycelium is like the Earth's WiFi system, sending signals and sharing nutrients. When you see a mushroom, even a little puffball, will you think of all that is invisible?" Jules allowed that question to hang in the air. "The end."

Silence hung heavy and the wind blew overhead. Her friends had gone down into the Earth with her to visit a tree, their favorite tree. The women looked at one another, the teens began to stretch and stir. "After inviting me back into my body, Karie asked me to wiggle my toes. She left as magically as she had appeared, but she gave me an enormous gift: Cooperation is our new civics." Her voice trailed off.

"I didn't know Karie could lead such a journey," Kate said. "We have a couple of shamanic practitioners in Boundary County too. It seems like an awesome time to learn about how trees communicate. Here's a word for you climate scientists—biomimicry. We could practice mimicking trees by talking more, just like this, rooted to one place. Trees are in constant communication with each other. I am going to invite Grey, my new husband, to come to the tipi next week, if that's alright with you. He's been a soil scientist all his life. He would love this circle."

After that, everyone wanted to talk at once. Samantha allowed the noise to fill the tipi. "I'm about to roll Jules home but mark your calendars: March 21, Saturday morning at 10. The mayors are convening their councils together. We will practice Civic Cooperation. Spread the word. Tell your Facebook and Instagram friends. Let's bring our signs and fill the auditorium.

Most of the elders said their goodbyes and slipped out the opening. The boys helped Sam close the flaps on the tipi hole. Turning their propane heater off signaled a quiet time for the hardy.

Chapter 12

DRAFTS AND RED INK

"Drawdown Scholars, what you are working on now are called drafts, because they are not in final form. After spring break, in mid-May, you will hand in your finished copies. I feel pride and excitement swelling like buds on fruit trees. Apologies to the trees, even though this is 100% recycled paper, it's still a tree." As Gail waved the pages, everyone could see all the red ink.

Each of the papers had a half sheet attached, signed by Gail with her signature heart and oxoxo. Rule 1: Become cooperative. Rule 2: Red marks are made with love. Rule 3: No outside comparison.

"Our first rule is cooperation: This is me being cooperative with you. Second rule—getting better can be painful, but no one should take my red marks personally. Third rule—none of will you compare yourself with any others. You become a better writer by comparing yourself to yourself, that's all." Gail let this sink in.

Finally, stirring the energy of shock, Gail said, "On May 1st you will make your teammates each a copy, four copies. Right? We will all use red pens. Okay? She passed out their pages, neatly stapled and severely marked with red ink. "I could have used a pencil like my mentor did. When I edit my own work, I like the red better, it's just easier to see." She waited.

They really were stunned, and Alex began to cry, "No one ever cared enough to mark my pages like this."

"Yeah," they all agreed.

Each Scholar read through every mark. In the few minutes it took, Gail went into the kitchen to make a phone call. There was no hospital bed anymore and Jules was walking with a cane, but they all felt at home here. Gail knew the reason was all the talking and laughter and tears they had shared. Each meeting, each sharing, made them stronger cooperators as a Circle.

Like a true Cancer with Virgo Rising, Sara had made a whiteboard calendar of events and meet-ups showing the next three months. She took a minute to make some marks. "We didn't know about this date, May 1st. That feels a bit scary. You love me, right? I am working hard for you." She started a chain hug and when Gail came back into the room, she found the girls folded around each other laughing.

Gail wrapped her arms around the knot of girls. "Remember when we pretended to be architects, as though we knew how this would go? We still don't know. But we want to see and feel the finish line. There's still a hundred choices to make."

Jules hadn't said much but suddenly beamed with gratitude. "Thank you so much Gail. Right. The final paper. Our presentations. Seeing red." She emphasized her marks by fanning the pages in the air. "Well there is so much red here, but we're on the right track. Aren't we?" There it was, the teenage voice of doubt.

Always the cheerleader, Alex answered. "More now than ever we're on the right track. I love what I am learning about Women and Girls in our bioregion."

Dot and Sara chorused together, "I love what I am learning." They laughed and linked pinkie fingers.

With this patter, Jules continued. "I like the idea of choices. Every day there seem to be two choices for everything. As Drawdown Scholars, what do we have choices about? How do we present to the mayors and councils? What order do we do it? Should we take time to debrief the Consultants' Circle or should we talk about what we learned by writing our paper? And for our school presentation slot, do we choose to be first team or last?" She pointed where Sara had just written Slot # on four sticky notes. The Dean had sent notices to their AP-STEM director. Presentation slots during AP class time spanned two weeks near the bottom of Sara's calendar.

Alex continued when Jules paused. "When do we ask for interviews with the Reader reporters? I have always wondered about Ben Olson, wasn't that Lyndsie Kiebert who came to our middle school presentation? Would we, I mean could we, ask them to interview us? It feels presumptuous. I want it to be their idea. Let's invite them to the Consultant's Circle, see what they say. When do we put out our official press release, so the Bonner Daily Bee readers get clued in? How are we going to control this thing once word gets out about our plan? When do we plan to go public? In the tipi, Sam said, we all need to learn leadership."

Dot raised her hand. "Wow! You just did a question-storm with yourselves. Let's take the questions, all good, one at a time. I don't feel like we need to debrief the Consultants' luncheon: it was totally wonderful. We spent one whole meeting already deciding that our order flowed with our pie chart; it makes lots of sense but really, the order doesn't matter.

"Here's my brainstorm: I would like to talk about what I learned writing down my Regeneration ideas. I've been talking a lot to Alex's dad, Joe, because he is so passionate right now. We keep running into each other at the library. Some of what I've written here are Joe's ideas. I want to give him credit. How do I indicate personal interviews?

"Speaking of credit, did you know there is a company called Nori that will pay our farmers to store carbon in their pastures? It can be measured! They are creating a carbon credit marketplace for carbon removal. I have learned so much by putting my nose on the keyboard and just typing."

Interrupting and apologizing, Alex said, "My dad likes talking to you, too. It's almost like he has changed completely, he's headed for a new career. I heard him tell Grandpa, what bugs him the most is learning leadership.

"Okay, so what I learned by doing inventory of Women and Girls surprised me. I discovered a group of moms who get together so their tiny toddlers can play. Another group meets at the library while their kids sit on the floor looking at pictures in books and teach each other words. These are fun to write about.

"I discovered open-mic night. There are women writers and poets we don't know much about. They show up at open mic every month and read to each other. These struggling artists could be our smallholders, they need a little grant money, about $1,000 each, to publish their work. We need our artists right now—when I went to open mic, I laughed and cried." Everyone smiled at Alex. With a Pisces Moon on her Pisces ascendant, water turns on inside of her easily. "Other smallholders will grow our local food if we ask them. Lots of kids are coming out of the school garden programs wanting a half-acre for themselves."

Sara jumped in because Alex was catching her breath. "You're probably not done, but I would like to speak a little about fear. We are the dreamers. For this to be real, we need lots of people to be talking like this. We are informed, action oriented. Jon says, the meeting on Spring Equinox will change our lives forever. We have a choice right now—to go for it, land this big tuna—or quit, short of a miracle. I want to learn to be the architect of a miracle. I am excited every night when I go to bed."

They all needed a breather, so Gail called for a break. When they came back together, they turned down the sound on their phones and seemed unsure of where their thread had been left. Gail would be the weaver here. She looked each girl straight in the eye. "Can I confess?" This question got their attention immediately.

"Did you see that trick? Emotional drama got your attention. Leadership is about getting and holding attention. When we lead with our emotions, everyone feels the authenticity of our words. Remember this when you plan for the mayors and councils, emotionally connected intelligence is the most human kind. All those folks also have very short attention spans. Most of them aren't trained listeners, but feeling is primal." She stood up to prowl around the room, thinking best on her feet.

"Each of you is the leader of your Sector, the only expert in town." Gail opened her journal to the pie chart. "Your expertise comes from documenting everything you've learned. For academia ... that's all good." Gail emphasized *academia,* the word nobody ever uses, and that was the end of her thoughts about expertise. She knew she had a fertile environment, so she planted her seeds carefully.

"By cultivating cooperation, we share into a deeper trough where there are no experts. On this team, short term and long term, we look for gifts locked inside of people, young and old. Self, first. When you get back from spring break," pointing to the calendar at the first week of April, "your world will expand out to the science community in your school. Finding gifts hidden inside of people feels almost holy."

Weaving the hearts and minds of her team, Gail continued. "Keep your eye on all your choices. This is leadership. Jules asked brilliant questions that need to be addressed. Thanks to Sara's leadership, you have transcripts of every meeting. Pay attention to questions because inquiry itself indicates leadership. To lead this community into a higher version of itself, use your spider web metaphor. Can you make the cascading benefits visible? Where do things connect? What are you weaving? We may not achieve Drawdown for a few years, but without your cooperating leadership—sharing your skills at weaving and connecting with the greater community—it will not happen at all.

"Before we plan for the mayors' presentation, what are your thoughts about spring break?" Gail knew this was a way to bring the girls back into controlling the conversation.

Dot raised her hand. "Seems like I am the party planner." She offered a smile that began shy and small with her head down, then morphed into a Cheshire Cat with her claws out. "Gail, we were going to invite you. After a lot of texting, everyone has decided to load up in a 10-seater van and go together to Escalante or somewhere. Dex is helping me on this one." Dot pointed to Sara.

Organization was Dot's Virgo thing. Of course, play figured into their grand design. That's why the school district emphasizes break, spring break spanned ten days. Poor play—Gail could hear the words of her old mentor: The natural heart of work is play. "Congratulations for learning so quickly about the importance of play." Gail grinned back like a Cheshire. "Roar," showing air claws.

"Wait!" Alex practiced the method of a drama-burst. "What were you wanting to confess?"

"I confess that I have been excited, too, especially early in the morning. A pair of owls have been waking me up. They seem like messengers, so I am searching for their message. Something about the end of February."

"Listen, Scholars, begin to feel again. Take long walks alone. Go in silence to a secret place and share your feelings with a tree. If you need snowshoes to get there, that's all the better. The deep snow quiet always thrills me. Go without a device. Ask yourself what you want to know about your subjects. Find the location inside of you where curiosity meets passion. What feelings connect to your subjects?

"This is such an important time. Ask Masai about leadership. Probably you all need a break to do art. Invite Linda and Maria to the tipi. Maybe a lyrical poem to nature or a soulful song wants to emerge from you. Being smart can become a hard driver in our brains. Grow up playful."

"You've practiced Drawdown presentations with the middle school and with the Consultants. The mayors are just the next ones. Each time, you polish your presentation more than the last time. You four teens are the only ones in town who know about reversing global warming. Over break you need to let your families know what role they might play. See if you can discover their hidden gifts."

These were good words; the room had been so full of words. Gail was almost finished. "Kenny and I are on our own getaway. Yay! I just found a gap for Oregon. Kenny's been thinking about places along the Oregon coast he wants to paint. Personally, I want to walk in drippy woods and see the early spring. We'll be away for a couple of weeks but I'm on Hotspot.

"Officially, I will see you on Friday March 20 for rehearsal updates and of course I will be wearing my finest to be with you on Saturday morning. Will someone get us in there, into the Sandpoint Event Center for our early Saturday meet-up? Wow." Gail blew kisses and reached up, wiggled her fingers out the door just like she had seen Gran do a few times; it was quite effective.

Chapter 13

AGNESS ROAD—THE MOTHER TREE

Everyone respected Gail's time away. Finally, after a few days she sent a group text: *"Is everyone OK?"* The reply-all responses were yes or 100% and that was that.

Going to the woods with Rosie was a necessity. She felt only a tiny bit more woke than her Scholars. Like parenting, mentoring requires a peek into the spiritual realm. Gail's inner-eye always takes care not to pry into daily details. Gail summoned her Coyote humor. Instantly a bell curve appeared, in the sky or in her head, she wasn't sure. The quiet, spiritual quality of deep dark woods always turned her mind on. Every young person needs a free-play walk into the woods.

She sighed. Such explorations were too rare. Two months before, when the young Scholars had loaded up her inbox, they were needy. As a team they had formed a solid, working core. Intense mentoring back then had risen to a crescendo. If the energy was placed on a bell curve, they had reached a natural peak together. Off the far side, that high energy began to drop like petals from a rose. Naturally. Quietly. Now those Scholars had each other and their community of parents. They had become weavers.

Nothing came to her inbox. Gail played a little more with her images. The energy of Imbolc had been present in the teens. The quickening of all their early seed ideas had been like Earth's own seeds wiggling awake. Life inside of them had merely been a sleeping seed. To old women and gardeners, this awakening to the inside of life is known as "quickening."

Kenny and Gail enjoyed being old adventurers. When they returned to a place, it felt more relaxing. In the autumn of 2018, the Oregon coast had been their destination. Listening to the local news in Gold Beach, they had learned about fires up the Rogue River. Something about it seemed important so they made Gold Beach one of their destinations in 2020 as things began to thaw. Driving up the Rogue grew out of a wish.

At the River delta on October 15, Gail and Kenny had stood beside the road and watched a long parade of firetrucks and hotshot trucks race up Agness

Road. Waving and cheering, they stood as tourists, wondering about this response team. Problem fires like the Klondike, started by lightning, burned long and hot in Oregon that summer. Kenny telephoned one of his sisters: "Those crews we saw racing up the Rogue River had just come from there. The fire boundaries closest to the road flared out of control, again. I counted 20 trucks, each loaded with teams of firefighters."

That was all Gail knew. Being a tourist in 2018, she didn't know the story before or after. Three years earlier, she had transformed her life by leaving her little farm. Now she was more of an Earth witness—a shapeshifter and a watcher. Her watched area had been the entire West, needing to see the truth of climate change for herself: the effects, subtle damages to ecosystems, especially wildlife refuges, her low vision penetrated the spirit of each place she walked with Rosie.

She felt the raw truth of geography on this return to Gold Beach and the Rogue River. Loyalty to a place requires boundaries and geographic limitations. She had no boundaries, and this expanded her loyalty. She felt the growing responsibility of her part in the industrial-informational complex world. This caused pain that she reckoned with every day.

Her thoughts returned to the young women on the team. Drawdown Scholars. Gail had not even known it was possible to define a bioregion for Drawdown. Cooperative mobilization among people was the only way to help the Earth heal herself. Letting the Project rest a week, she coaxed herself outside.

Nature captivates. Inner Coyote had a good laugh at this thought. Gail knew this was not true for everyone. Through one of her big changes in midlife she lived in the woods. During that dramatic and deep three-year Passage, she taught herself to release every thread of her former corporate life and connections. Ego transformed into humility when her Graduate Mentor taught the soul's journey toward God through Hell, Purgatory and Heaven from Dante's Trilogy. Pride still made her feel a pang of something. Guilt?

Personal evolution progressed to nature connection. Coyote was in charge. Tracking and bird language became a long, beautiful new thread to follow. In 1998 an academic literature review introduced her to Jon Young. His quest wrapped Nature connection around Spirit connection. With Indigenous help, Jon taught how Spirit moves through self and others and flows into community connections. Always, Jon sends the learning challenge back outside. Gail lives through this connection. Medicinal plants came first. Birds came next. Sacred Stones create a niche for her elder years.

Her spiritual assignment always returns to mentoring. Beautiful people spread out all over—some stayed only a season, others transformed into everlasting relations. She knows about the human spirit and how growing pains stretch us. Astrologically, our growing edge is the North Node. Both Nodes of the Moon, usually accurate signatures, guide our emotions.

Walking through the forest, staying mostly on the trail, loosened knots in Gail's brain and body. Her movements became slower, until she heard a tree. This beauty sat back 30' off to the left side. Gail thought, "Left is feminine. You're one of the Mother Trees." This was her simple greeting before she reached out to touch a sunny sliver of bark.

MOTHER TREE

Cedar. Western Red, they say. Mother, I say.
When I touched the shredded bark,
A shot of electric current greeted me. Noticeable, but not harmful
I looked over my shoulder, and up to see how Sun penetrated these woods.
Here is power. Wisdom. 300 years old.

Ten minutes to walk around this Cedar, listening, kissing, dreaming.
I spread my arms and placed my breasts against her bark.
The way to channel 300 years of wise experience is to ask questions;
This is where relationship begins.
"What do you think, Great Mother? Are humans going to continue?"
Coyote knew to be blunt, direct.
"Not in their current configuration,
Humans will not get through their grief unless they grow close in spirit,
Closer to Trees. You could show the way, old woman."

The spirits were laughing. "It's true. Losing capacity sharpens other abilities."
This is the elder learning curve: I received Tree's gifts.
"Capacity has no limits grief will be endless.
Dance for me," Tree asked.
Knees not what they used to be, hips ... oh dear Goddess.
"Would you settle for a little waltz, Mother Cedar?"
I danced a merry-go-around with Mother Tree,
Emptying and allowing joy to rise like the Moon.
Reversed directions and watched joy set like the Sun,
Looking up and looking down. Celebrating and honoring
With little rituals, this is the way forward.
Crow cawed. "Hello to you too, Crow."
"You are my people." It was true.
"You are all Ancestors of each other, you left Crows behind to call your name."
"How many people have danced for you, Cedar?"
None for 50 years, before that, only a few.

Divine thoughts flowed from this Tree.
I began to weep, a gift of moment or grief?
"All things simultaneous."
I lay out full body to touch my length to the Earth and spread my arms wide.

After the Scholars declared their passions and followed their inner threads, they discovered what happens when light shines on something. It blooms. Through writing, the petals of their flowers reached for the Sun. Every woman on the team felt her limitations stretch every day. The doubt and inner critic of their pre-teens fell away. January and February had been an intense time.

Gail allowed these thoughts to flow as she relaxed on the ground and offered a hug to the Earth. Rosie stepped up to lick the salty tears and laid down too. Looking skyward in the dark woods, "This is why I work with young people," she thought. "I want them to feel this."

Why was she all alone in these woods? Mother Cedar spoke: "People have not remembered what you know, what has taken you 70 years to remember. We heal Souls, Mother Earth and I, but connection and surrender must be present before we can do any good. People need to bring their humility as you have done. They need to come with open-hearted curiosity."

Returning to her journal, Gail wrote: "This is serious shit. We have been here before. We are Ancestors of each other. When a Circle forms, those who sit together have a Soul imprint that knows about connection. That is why women sit together. The men's movement is catching up—Kate and Grey's wedding—all those beautiful people sitting in circles together.

The next day and the next, Gail returned to Mother Cedar to lay down on Mother Earth, uphill and downhill. The sky was drippy one day and blue the next. "Take this energy back to your people. Ask them. Invite them to remember. If they can imagine a better world, it means they are beginning to remember."

Rosie loved the trail more than lying around, so down they skipped to-gether. Gail needed her 10,000 steps; she had been getting only half that. Her mentor's spirit had awakened to the realization, the remembrance that Mother Earth had once been covered with trees. Complex dark forests had blanketed all North America except the deserts and the prairies.

How could people be reminded of this? Gail knew it was a spiritual con-nection that did not include any religious figureheads. The experience of the dark, drippy woods was life support for Animal Others. Humans owe their ear-liest learning-curve to bears—people do get excited when they see bears, but they cannot remember why. Being omnivorous, bears were original teachers for finding food in the forest.

Gail's journey to the Rogue was all it needed to be. She offered her hair as thanksgiving in a Stone ceremony before she left. Her tears had touched Mother Cedar. She had received her bear-story to share. From these wet woods, Gail's spirit was refreshed, and she felt grateful.

Chapter 14

COUNCIL CIRCLES AND STONE CEREMONIES

Old women practice listening.
Inner spirit. Outer spirit.
Seeking answers.
Then we celebrate the Earth with a ceremony.
Kneeling on the Earth is a Divine honor.

Long emails with new inspirations about their presentations to the mayors showed up in Gail's inbox. She was happy to be back from Oregon and have the time to sense the Scholars building energy through slides and images in the PowerPoint Sara had delivered. In paragraphs she'd received, Gail electronically tweaked what they shared using track-changes online, user-friendly, no paper needed. Still marked in red. They had taken time to edit one another and what Gail saw looked polished and professional. Through comments in the margins, Gail only reminded about a connection or a thread for weaving.

Her chest swelled with love and admiration. Along with directions to continue practice sessions on video, Gail suggested that one or two parents have a read and offer comments. Ms. Yost reviewed their academic drafts and only wanted to know version # and word count before spring break. Each girl had a 10-minute office visit with her and left smiling.

Even though her Scholars wanted to go straight to a pre-rehearsal meeting, Gail redirected them inside the tipi. The energy was low, sleepy and warm. "Wakey, wakey," Gail laughed, carrying Stones for ceremony. "We practice someone else's ritual until we find our own." She placed her Irish green shawl, folded square, in the center and looked up through the tipi hole. "Great Spirit, we ask you to send our Ancestors. We need help."

Gail emptied her bags of stones out onto the four corners. "Earth has been very generous to share her abundance." She felt the energy rise, curiosity replaced nervous energy or anger or indifference. The number of teens had doubled in a month. Kneeling over the cloth and her Stones, Gail created a Circle that touched the edges of the cloth. "Let's go around, each of you pick a stone, say something you are grateful for and place the stone inside this circle, anywhere."

Setting the energy to go Sun-wise, Jason picked up a stone. "You said wakey, wakey and I realize I am not. But I am grateful." As the group shared being grateful for their Ancestors, for the Earth, and for #FridaysforFuture time in the tipi, the elder spirits who were present held the edges and began to glow. They stood like sentinels with arms and palms open, listening deeply. Gail made eye contact with Laura, Maria, Masai, with J'nell and Victoria.

Gail picked up a stone. "Aren't we brilliant together? I feel gratitude for you, for the elders here, and for another round. As a gift to the tipi speak one sentence about your growing edge." She swirled an arm around in a complete circle, "Everything is alive. When you open your heart, everything hears you. Your growing edge refers to your curiosity. What are you most interested in?"

Gail sat in one of the empty chairs and invited her friends to do the same. Masai made a gesture of reaching out from her heart. Everyone was in this ritual together. How simple it was. Laura leaned in to light a few candles she had in her pocket. The altar continued to grow and began to glow.

Picking up a stone with a face, Gail said, "I am interested in wrapping my friends—young and old—in a Council Circle. We have gifts to polish and we need to practice deep listening." Passing her Stone the other direction, "Will you find a place for my stone?" And so it went, everyone shared and passed their stone for their neighbor to place. Before they were finished, everyone felt the healing energy of deep listening.

Gail was struggling to get to her feet when Ben jumped up to give her a hand and received a hug. "This is a gift for the community. You have just experienced a ritual. It was organic, spontaneous and rose from the Earth. Any one of you can repeat this anytime, anywhere. Gather a few stones and begin."

The generations came together offering hugs to each other. "Knowledge is not reversible: once you know, you cannot not know," she said.

Jules stood and began putting stones back into their bags. "I'm getting stronger every day. Our team is going to take Gail to our pre-rehearsal meeting. See you all there tomorrow when we present to the mayors."

Masai uncrossed her knees from the lotus posture. "I will come next week and pass this stone to reveal another layer of Council energy."

J'nell spoke last, "Council Circles like this one that you kids started, they will be the only way through the mess of the world. Keep it up."

The hours sitting in group protest were good for lots of things. Taking the whole day to sit happened only in the beginning. Now, kids came around in two-hour shifts and made a reason to leave. Council may help them stay interested in their futures as the protest intended.

Outside, the Scholars could see their breath in the air. "Mom told me about the work you have done with ceremony," Dot looked at Gail. "I like it. Can we do that more often, can we do it as a team?"

Alex jumped in. "Will you tell us a story? You were gone a long time."

Jules raised her hand, and everyone laughed because she was holding Gail's. "We missed you, but we were terribly busy playing. Were you playing too?"

Gail reached across the circle to place a finger under Sara's chin. "We have Sara's 0° Aries Moon to thank for the date of our next presentation. It is upon us. Are you ready, Beauty?" Sara had the most stunning blush, which rose suddenly.

"As soon as you tell me that you're feeling good about where you stand, if you're ready to open your ideas to the community, then I will share a story about why."

Alex had more to say. "There are so many loggers upset with my dad's decision to quit logging. There's been a lot of grief around our kitchen table these past two weeks. That grief is not coming from Dad, just everyone who visits. He's being weighed down feeling his way through guilt and abandonment. I think he needs a shrink to get him through this."

That was more information than she had shared with her teammates. "I may not be going on break with you guys, I can't pay my share." Gail felt a new quiet descend like a blanket on their small circle. Gail raised her arm and pointed toward Monarch Mountain Coffee. "To the coffee shop! I'm buying coffee, tea or chocolate for everyone. We have some logistics to sort through."

Sara and Jules ordered Zinger Tea, Dot wanted French Roast with lots of room for cream and Alex wanted hot chocolate. Gail asked for a double Yerba Mate. They resumed their tight circle around one of the back tables. When Gail set down her tea, she surveyed the room. The only tense energy was right there.

Gail reassured the Scholars. "Our fundraising will begin at the meeting with the mayors and their city councils. Your share of spring break expenses will be covered, Alex. It's really important for our soaring spirits to play together, I get that.

"Listen. Here's a little story to draw us into our bodies again: I wandered up a trail along the Rogue River from Gold Beach until I heard something. A tree. A Mother Tree talked to me. She reminded me what we've been forgetting. She asked me to dance for her." Gail looked around and realized there was no resistance to her words at all.

"First, we all need to dance, every day, dance and sing too. This brings joy and that's one of the missing ingredients in the world today. Everyone is uptight and worried. Joy took a stage-left exit. Begin with yourselves—when you're sitting around a desert fire, shivering, get up and dance! That is an ancient way of being."

She softened her eyes to see the spirit of the story, "The Mother Tree told me how 200 years of forgetting has almost completely destroyed the forests. I realized the energy of Mother Earth had given me my rhythm. Try lying on the Earth and listening. Polly Higgins called this *earthing*. It is the most wonderful feeling! I went three days in a row to lay on the ground with Mother Earth and to dance around her Mother Tree."

"On the last day, Rosie and I saw a bear cross the trail in front of us and we fell down like dead. Bear could have cared less about us. She was just there to help me remember that being human has been a very long journey of learning how to be one with the world. Seems we learned and then forgot again."

As the girls listened deeply Gail harvested something from the bear she didn't know was there. "Find your animal ally in your dreamtime during spring break. Who else is important enough to receive our attention, our love, and our protection? I want to hear about your animal allies, any animal encounters you've had. We will have some time for play, beginning right now." She raised her teacup high and the young women joined her. "Cheers."

Sara directed everyone's attention back to the rehearsal. "We actually do need to talk about tomorrow."

Chapter 15

THE HEART REVEALED

Mayor Shelby Rongstad had pulled off something good. The Event Center Auditorium was packed and like all small towns, people were glad to see one another. After he acknowledged the other mayors and thanked them for coming, he joked that the snowslide across the road to the ski hill probably helped attendance this morning. The avalanche had made it easier for everyone to be present, Saturday being a usual ski day for working folks.

"I want to thank Sara Best-Jewell, an AP student at Sandpoint High School, for instigating this presentation. The team of young women calling themselves Drawdown Scholars say we will have something to talk about when they are finished with their presentation. Sara's father, my friend Jon Jewell, calls them Climate Solutionaries. That has a little zing to it, don't you think? Maybe each of them has her own cape. I present to you the Drawdown Scholars." Mayor Rongstad held the mic out to one of them and Sara wrestled with her notes.

Behind the Scholars onstage, two images were projected in split-screen. Half was the book image, *Drawdown: The Most Comprehensive Plan Ever Proposed to Reverse Global Warming* which is powerful on its own and the other half were the 4 Sectors the girls had studied.

As Sara stepped up to the mic, the audience lowered their voices. Sara used the familiar because the mayor was like family. "Mayor Shelby, thanks for your introduction." Sara introduced the Student Council from Sandpoint High who knew to stand and take their cheers. This demonstrated good follow-up by Clark Fork, Priest River, and Bonners Ferry Student Councils. "We all invited you, but it was my idea first, so here we go." Sara blushed and continued through a self-imposed bluster she had wanted to avoid.

Gail glanced at her phone, that took only five minutes. The mayors had front row seats and their city council members sat all around and behind. Gail didn't know a single one of them; this was her first problem, she realized.

Holding the mic, Sara trembled a little as she introduced her team members. "Seventeen! That is the age of each one of the team members up here, and the number of Solutions we're presenting. Out of 100 Solutions identified in this book, we chose 17, easily there could be quite a few more. We found these Solutions already here and working in Bonner and Boundary counties. This is the beauty of Drawdown Solutions: They are sourced from the familiar—a plan found or discovered rather than invented."

Sara clicked to show the 17 Solutions that had been chosen then clicked the next slide, where people could examine their topo of the two counties. Sara introduced the Scholars. "Here to tell you about our bioregion is my esteemed teammate, Alex Olson. Presenting about our Food Networks and how to strengthen those systems is Jules Pergosi. After we hear from Dot Andrus about Land Use, I will share about Climate Justice. My name is Sara Best-Jewell."

Someone had told Sara that she was more fairy-like every day, so she adopted her inner fairy and spread her arms to reveal big wing sleeves. "They say we are gathered here because I chose this date. We are also gathered here because Mayor Shelby works out with my Dad, Jon. I am proud to say both of my dads are here today. If you've eaten at the Hoot Owl or Joel's, you might know my dad, Dex Best. It is my pleasure to introduce our mentor hiding behind the scenes, Gail Burkett. Her topic is Rights of Nature. My topic Climate Justice connects to Gail's. She and I will go last."

Sara handed the mic to Alex who clicked the next slide showing the forest service map that so many people depend on to locate a road or a trail into the woods. "Here is our bioregion. Most of our 56,675 people in these 3,192 square miles have our hands full. We are over-busy because cooperation and community support have hit low points. I've been from border to border, all around the edges and the interior with my dad, Joe." He raised his hand from an aisle seat three rows back on the wing.

"Inside these boundaries I searched for the participants in my topic, Women and Girls. I heard about their stress and busy-ness in every township, in the baby and toddler groups, and every library reading group. I learned where the women hang out, who they are and all the good works they do to raise their families. I appreciated my mother, Deborah, raising four children in the prime years of her life. I found weavers, sewers, knitters, some tending goats, sheep, alpacas and babies while creating their hand crafts and home canning for the winter.

"There are lots of gardeners and farmers here, there are businesswomen selling retail and wholesale. Think of the Miller family who buy wholesale and sell retail and bake for us. We have healers, midwifes and herbalists. We have poets, artists, and authors. Besides taking a thorough inventory of all that we have here, our goal is to sort and collate needs that every woman speaks about.

"Women need state-sponsored daycare so they can do their work. We need forest schools for the little ones so they will grow up connected to nature. When you change the local law about canning as a cottage industry, much more food will appear from the women's kitchens."

Clicking a new slide, Alex said, "I prepared this list as a hand-out. Women of our bioregion have asked for these things particularly. Our strength will rise through cooperatives for our basic needs. Each one of these categories represents new jobs, even new industries inside our bioregion."

- Food Co-ops
- Tiny Houses
- Daycare
- Small Loans
- Retraining
- North Idaho College Courses
- Community Kitchen Restoration: Cottage Industry Food Prep
- Teens in the Tipi: Rights of Passage Ceremonies and More Visitors
- Instruction on Self-reliance, a Segment of the Green New Deal

"Adding the teens in the tipi felt important, since society doesn't know what to do with us. We are growing up faster, with all eyes on our Generations, Z and pulling along the babies we call the Alphas. We appreciate the irony of being last and first, the end and a new beginning.

"There is plenty to do here. I want to introduce to you Jules Pergosi who has studied our Food System Sector. As you will see, Food overlaps other Sectors—the whole map actually."

Alex sat down to resounding applause. She half stood and took a little bow before settling back down.

Slowly gathering herself and her thoughts, Jules accepted a chair from Alex close to the edge of the stage. "Maybe you heard about my leg," Jules began. "I shattered my tibia the day after Christmas—I'm a miracle!"

Jules used a little more drama to turn attention to Food. She pulled back her hair with one hand and leaned over her mic, making eye contact with the audience. "You plan on eating three times today, right? Do you know where all that food comes from? Here in north Idaho we are food insecure for two reasons: We don't grow enough of our own food and there is no warehouse supplying our groceries. Idaho doesn't have a warehouse at all, did you know that?

"A story circulated in 1999 during the Y2K scare that if a pandemic rose, like Ebola or SARS, the borders would be closed. How secure will we be within our own borders? Alex overlaps here on women's needs for food security. We found all women's needs urgent, but you have the power to change the cottage industry laws—there is magic waiting in food canning for our security.

"Food relates to global warming in ways that surprised me. What does a *plant rich diet* mean? This means eating from the produce section and hardly ever visiting the middle sections or the meat sections of the store. It refers to our own agency, our nutritional choices, and how we teach the children about food. From this single Drawdown Solution, we see two more. Quite a lot of food is wasted in our bioregion. Nationwide it's more than 30% of the total amount grown, adding 8% to the overall pool of annual greenhouse gases. Why? How? What are we doing with all that waste and can we do better?

"Mayors, council members, we need policy in place and a cooperative system to divert all our wasted food to a single place. The answer to increasing our effectiveness lies squarely in your power. My mom, Robin Pergosi, and I talked with Waste Management. They helped Boise design a food waste system. They just need all of us to come along with new, big ideas suitable for your townships.

"I am going to put up this slide for just a moment." Two people appeared on screen. "This is Lynne Twist and Paul Hawken, our teachers from Drawdown Solutions. Jules slowed for emphasis. "They believe in this new perspective: Maybe global warming is not happening TO us, maybe it's happening FOR all of us. Global warming equals opportunities for innovation and personal growth. We need to wake up and become a human family again. When I first heard their words, I cried. Then I stopped feeling sorry for myself and got to work.

"Because I was confined to bed and couldn't visit you, I called many of you. Everyone answered questions about food—grocery managers, gardeners, and farmers. I learned tons and maybe I was lucky to be in my hospital bed all the way through January and half of February. Some good growers reminded me about photosynthesis, what begins to happen when a seed germinates. I was in the Northside School Garden Club that Gail directed and I learned the value of seeds."

Jules leaned over her mic again and began to whisper. "Just a little story … One year we let the carrots go to seed. They grew gorgeous big umbels this high off the ground." She stood up straight and held her hands way over her head. She eased back into her chair. "Okay I was just a kid then, they seemed taller because they grew from our nice big raised beds. The flowers grew right out of the carrot. If you live in a city, you probably don't know about carrot seeds, but we helped start the seed library here at the Sandpoint Library from those carrot seeds. We grew enough for the whole bioregion.

"You can search through *Drawdown.org* for information on all of these Solutions." She flipped the slide to enlarge the Food Sector.

"In your handouts, we offer the whole list with highlighted selected Solutions. There are 20 Solutions in the Food Sector alone! Researchers discovered half of these Solutions play a role in releasing carbon and the other half store carbon. When the Solutions are fully functional, carbon begins to rebalance. Most of you know my math genius dad, Jordi. Through the miracle of mathematics, he helped me to understand a gigaton of carbon dioxide!"

Jules was excited, getting to the heart of her talk. She wanted to stand, but Gail stepped behind her and whispered, "It's okay to sit."

Taking a deep breath to gather herself, Jules started again. "Kids are taught about responsibility. Every human is responsible. Right here we are responsible for our miniscule share of global warming and we can become one of the first bioregions accountable to reverse the damage and degradation for Bonner and Boundary counties. And, this news flash—farmers can now enter the carbon marketplace and get paid for storing carbon."

Jules took a breath waiting for her message to sink in. Other than the student body, she had never stood in front of a crowd before. She wondered, were they judging her? "A circle of women appeared in the tipi to support us—we called them Consultants. They say we have created a rural model for at least 3,192 other counties in the U.S. We will begin with the other 42 Idaho counties.

"This new path forward involves talking and cooperating, knitting our eight local communities together in a dozen new ways." A large and intricately beautiful spider web appeared on the screen. "Drawdown researchers have written that these Solutions can create an Agricultural Renaissance—a transformation of food-growing practices that bring people to regeneration and bring abundance back to the land. We will use biomimicry to do like spider knows best."

"We're only 17 years old but we learned we can reverse global warming. Yeah, that's right, let those words sink in. We can draw those greenhouse gases back down into the soil and into trees planted. We can reverse the damage done to Planet Earth in the past 100 years, but we need to cooperate on these Solutions. As a bioregion of cooperating people, we will find our own Solutions. As a community, we need to change policy about food and grow enough for our own food security. The ways are open for discussion and for experimentation. We want to feel part of the human family right here. We think," waving at her friends, "action feels better than anxiety.

"My ask for those of you sitting on the city council is that you hire Diane

Green to work this Food Sector into local-local laws that will make us more secure. The Extension Agents are both here, Jennifer Jensen and Kate Painter: They have identified the inadequacy in our food system and need your help. Thank you for being here."

Even though Jules didn't feel she had finished strong, the audience applauded appreciatively. She stood and bowed while Gail pulled her chair back into the group row and offered a balancing hand. She sat and accepted a little hug.

Dot took the mic. "I am Dot Andrus and my family lives off the land up Flume Creek, which flows into Rapid Lightning Creek. The whole fandamily has lived up there for more than 100 years. Traveling to and from town, most of our contribution to this climate chaos has come through emissions. When the ancestors used a horse and buggy, it took so long, they only came down once a month. During the winter, maybe not at all, but their old sleighs are still in the barn along with the old crocks that they used to make sauerkraut. Can you believe, we buy sauerkraut now?

"We worry every year about fire, about rain, and trees turning orange from bark beetles. We worry that there's not enough water content in our snow. These worries come from global warming. Our ancestors only worried about lightning fires."

She clicked on her first slide after the spider web. It returned to an adaptation of Alex's topo of the bioregion. "I have spent days in the county clerks' office to discover what this forest service map really means. All my life, we've had one of these in every vehicle, haven't you? White indicates private ownership; the yellow overlay shows plowed fields. Those are most often heavily grazed after the grass grows high and the cut comes off around July 1. Green indicates forest or land held in trust for the people by state and national governments. The blue shows clear cuts. We are looking at 100% of this bioregion, 3,192 square miles." Dot clicked on a new slide.

"Cropland. Grassland. Forestland. Wetland: These are common to every bioregion in the Pacific Northwest. We have no Desertland, not yet. We do not dare imagine two or three degrees of warming. Desert is the single strongest threat to our bioregion and it's as close as the Bruneau Sand Dunes and the Craters of the Moon Monument near Idaho Falls. The desert has creeped up the Salmon River to Riggens and into Lewiston. Land managers measure desert-creep and animal migrations. We have the intellect to examine our lands. Why wouldn't we? On this map, all of the green belongs to the people and all of the blue is degraded.

"Laura Parsons from the clerks' office helped me with this. Please raise your hand, Laura. We also found 45 abandoned parcels of land, most of them with abandoned buildings on them." Dot's next slide was back to Alex's topo with small black areas colored in. "I would like to suggest that you mayors have real power here. You could convince the counties to contact these absent owners to offer a deal: Maybe we could cancel taxes or make a Land Trust agreement. You absolutely could take these parcels by eminent domain for the people of our two counties. Out of 2,460,080 total acres, they may look inconsequential, 40-acre parcels mostly including one that was 100 acres. In the audience we have students who have participated in the elementary school garden projects who want ½ acre of their own. Imagine!

"With these 2,000 acres, we can put about 1,000 people to work, first in restoration and then in helping us become much more food secure. We will need to retrain loggers—they could help lead this project. We definitely have people moving here from coastal areas already. Who will write community grants for domes and high tunnels?" She clicked through a few photo slides and stopped on Gail Burkett's geodesic dome. "We could be growing food on the back side of the calendar like people do throughout New England. We have the water resources."

The next slide showed the Land Use Sector with 4 Solutions highlighted.
- Indigenous Peoples Land Management
- Aforestation
- Forest Protection
- Biochar

"These huge topics are what I have been working on. I share these Solutions with you because I need your help. We have a lot to learn from Indigenous People. We all live on land previously occupied by Spokane, Kootenai, Nez Perce, and Coeur d'Alene tribes. When we present to the student body, we will ask for opening prayers and blessings by these tribal leaders.

"Another 1,000 jobs are coming to our bioregion to replant and care for new forest plantings. We invited the Native Plant Society here today, please raise your hands. You will help take us beyond tree planting to the Solution called *Aforestation*. We want our forests back."

Dot used the photo from Alex's trip to the St. Joe. "2019 was a record year for the cut coming off. This is not something to be proud of; there were thousands of displaced animals who thrived in those places. We are in a climate emergency. Seeing this kind of devastation anywhere in Idaho creates local shame. Believe me, the loggers are not benefiting economically. They say they are barely able to make ends meet. Help me rethink this whole system. This is my most urgent ask. Let's expand growing food and trees through these 45 abandoned sites."

A slide highlighting biochar appeared on the screen. It was a lone word floating in a cloud-filled sky. "This one belongs to our team: We have already formed an LLC. Jon Jewell is our attorney. He came to the tipi one day and we all signed. This is an entrepreneurial adventure led by the kids. Last fall when the slash piles were burned, our most valuable resource went up in smoke. That smoke hung around, beneath a pressure inversion, for a month. Our air quality was so awful it seemed forests were burning and increasing risk for asthma in little kids and everyone else. We ask you to write policy to make that totally illegal. This is our most urgent request. Throughout November it was so smoky, we felt shame and bewilderment; this must be stopped from happening ever again."

She clicked on another slide explaining biochar. "Before I stop, let's linger for a moment and see how many key words we recognize. Sawdust. Forestry. Organic waste. Deforestation. As always, there is more. Thank you." Dot admired her slide. It showed a portable kiln next to a slash pile. Below the photo were the words: **Slow burn, without oxygen=Biochar=Fertile soils for 1,000 years.**

"Since Sara introduced us, I get to tell you she is the leader of our team: Here again is Sara Best-Jewell."

"The beauty and bounty of our place on Earth," Sara changed the slide to the Blue Marble, "is one of millions of eco-systems. We Drawdown Scholars came here to take care of our little place on the planet. Since our team began studying this bioregion, and snowshoeing to our favorite hangout spots, we feel more related, like a deeper belonging is rooting us here. Every part of the Earth and our little slice of heaven right here feels more precious every day. Today we're talking about the carbon cycle: Either carbon is sequestered, held in a tree, or drawn down into the soil through photosynthesis. Or, like the emissions that delivered all of us here, that carbon escapes into the atmosphere."

Sara stepped to the edge of the stage and felt a little vertigo, so she took two steps back. Her knees were wobbly. She was still talking her way through stage fright. Masai had coached her and she could hear those words now: "Disarm the audience. Find one person to focus on and see them naked. You will feel less vulnerable."

"Climate Justice is my broad topic. Honestly, it dates back in time through words like environmental justice, air and water pollution. I am the diversity in this room. Consider what has been documented. Countless academic papers have been written about the consequences of degraded water and air for people just like me. I was born disadvantaged. Thanks to destiny perhaps, I was adopted into privilege. My greatest blessing comes to me through the deep taproots of my family. We are rooted in this place.

"But Climate Justice is the topic that most easily hides in communities like ours. Other people of color do live here, just not very many. Thousands of our citizens live on the edge of poverty. Climate has disproportionately affected women, Indigenous People and low-income families who visit the amazing soup kitchens we have in this community. For many, especially those closest to town, the soup kitchen may be their only meal for the day. More disadvantaged people will be arriving every month. They will need something from our abundance. Climate Justice identifies the hidden needs of the community, especially the lowest on the invisible social scale. On the flip side, Climate Justice identifies the generosity of a community."

Clicking on the slides, she showed sewer treatment plants in every township, the water system with all its parts. "I love Waterkeepers the most. Locals finally got the fluoride out of our water. What about the Walkable City sign at both ends of Sandpoint? Do we really have a walkable city? We need to make our city not only more walkable, we need to subsidize transportation to help those folks with fewer means of mobility, like those who come to the food kitchen. I propose we allow them to ride our Spot bus for free. I propose we make our Spot fleet electric ASAP. These ideas for you who make policy decisions are all outlined in your handout.

She flipped on her last slide. These were the specific asks she had found in just 10 weeks of looking:
- SPOT busses electrified
- Free bicycles
- Sidewalk projects
- 100s of victory gardens
- Tent accommodations in parks
- Homeless shelters
- Tiny houses

The applause had grown louder with each presenter. The energy of applause was welcome. Sara knew this was for the team and she gestured for the other three Scholars to stand up with her.

"Now we have a special guest. Our mentor Gail Burkett will close for us."

"Each one of our Drawdown Scholars did a marvelous job wrapping their chosen Sectors into our bioregion. My own topic peers far into the future." She clicked on a slide divided in four parts which showed local icons: an oil train crossing the lake; the Pend Oreille River; Schweitzer Mountain covered with snow; and, kids playing at City Beach. "To enable more of the good, cascading consequences from these mighty efforts of restoration, regeneration, and community cooperation, we need to plan for the residents we have and those who will migrate here because of climate.

"As I look around at this collective government body, I am in awe of the power you hold in your positions as our local elected officials. We want to give you time to talk over our ideas, so I leave you with one request: When you protect this bioregion with Rights of Nature, a powerful, new layer of protection will come from you, our local city and county officials." Words hung in the air as she scrolled slowly through scenes of rivers, big trees, animals, and pets. "You have the power to place actual legal protections on these precious things we all take for granted. The link to this organization, Community Environmental Legal Defense Fund, is in your handouts.

"I am here to introduce you to this Rights of Nature concept. On behalf of these young Scholars who represent the next generation, we ask you to place those protections that are within your power. Rights of Nature is spreading around the planet as the necessary protection for those without voices. We cannot take our water, our mountains or any of our public lands for granted anymore. The lake is threatened by Burlington Northern every day, Priest River is threatened by the smelter, and too many clear cuts have been hidden from our view.

"The beautiful protesting teens in the tipi have taught me one very powerful thing," Gail concluded. "We feel stronger together when we sit and talk. The kids are here to make sure you know your responsibility and your power to protect this place we all love."

Gail finished with a slide of the four Scholars strolling down the middle of a Sandpoint street, arm-in-arm. Then she stepped back as her team stepped forward. She took the hands of her team in a huddle and they all yelled "Love!" and threw love into the air with shouts and screams before taking a bow together.

While the applause rang out for the Scholars, Karen Lanphear took the stage and reached for the mic. "Bravo! Through the amazing technology of texting," she waved her phone high in the air, laughing, "I have just secured the Panida Theater so these Scholars can introduce their wonderful ideas to the community. Two events, Friday evening May 15 and Saturday afternoon May 16. In the handout you've all received, they've listed their phone numbers and emails. These are digital girls; they will answer the best they can. If they don't know the answer to your questions, they will search until they find it.

"We need to send them back to their studies for now. They finish their quarter before Memorial Day by presenting this AP-STEM Junior Project to their student body. The following two days, the Consultant's Circle will escort them to the other high schools for student body programs."

The Consultants rose from their seats and waved at the mayors. Like the fund-raising pros they were, each of them produced a folded bowl from her bag and passed them down the aisles. "Throw in $5, $10, or $20 to help these young women," Karen urged. "I booked the dates at the Panida and paid for them already. Save these dates—May 15 and 16. Let's give them another round of applause."

When the Consultants joined the Scholars at the back of the stage, J'nell counted her money, "Oh good, here's $80." Cindy said, "I have a total of $60, not bad."

Masai beamed, "I broke $100. That's gas money and carbon credits already paid for."

Alex wiped away her tears of joy. Gail did too and pulled out a yellow handkerchief to blow her nose. No one used Kleenex anymore, too many trees had given their lives already, and they all used bamboo in their bathrooms. Gail appreciated that Yokes and Winter Ridge carried the U.S.-made, Bim Bam Boo sustainably-sourced toilet paper made in the U.S. by Ecosentials. Phil Levin and his daughter Zoe said they stumbled across a troubling statistic. Each day, America, the number-one consumer of toilet paper, flushes 27,000 trees down the toilet. Toilet paper is a $14 billion industry in the U.S alone. They had talked about this: Bamboo is ranked #35 in Drawdown Solutions, but Dot and Sara argue over whether it is in Land Use or Materials.

"Let's regroup at Jules' house. Do you all have that address?" Gail asked the women who had been part of her Women's' Circle for years. She had her arms around Hattie who was blowing her nose too. "Oh! My God," Hattie said over and over. River was standing right there, dangling her keys, "Anyone else need a ride?" Gail reached for her hand, "Thank you Miss Daisy!"

Peering directly into Hattie's eyes while holding River's hand, Gail said, "Well, that turned out well. Can you come for our debrief session?" Hattie couldn't go and shook her head no. River said laughing, "Of course."

Looking around she could only see the backs of teens and elders going down the stage stairs. That route led directly outside. Reaching for an elbow, Gail asked in a low voice, "Please, Tina. Will you stay ten minutes to see what the crowd reaction is? We won't start without you."

Tina observed this scene from behind the curtain …

Dr. Nancy Gilliam was a woman with a plan: She had been a special invitee to today's presentation. In 2009 Nancy had attended Al Gore's first class, Climate Reality. She was now the most senior cohort in his 11 years of educating leaders. Her skills as a facilitator would harvest each of the "asks" made by the Scholars. This was an assignment she relished, especially since two county commissioners were in attendance.

Nancy sat down on the floor of the stage, dangled her feet over the edge and addressed the audience. "Hello. My name is Dr. Nancy Gilliam. Through my Climate Solutions University, I have helped 44 communities just like this one—in fact a decade ago we started here. It's time to bring that decade of deepening knowledge back home to this bioregion."

In 2007 and 2008, when the looming climate crisis had troubled many hearts in Sandpoint, a wonderful group had been formed, almost family. After two years of organizing and researching, the little network of concerned folks folded their organization into Dr. Nancy's non-profit, certain that she could carry their efforts forward. Now, Nancy was Gail's ace and an easy friendship to resume.

Mayor Shelby Rongstad and Nancy Gilliam had worked together for years; he thought she was his secret, just like Gail did. Mayor Shelby sat beside her on the stage, a little more awkward in Dr. Nancy's casual style—a more familiar approach than normal council meetings. She handed him the mic.

"Those young Scholars blew me away today. I couldn't be prouder of our school district and of you, their parents and friends. It truly takes a village to raise children." Shelby handed the mic back to Dr. Nancy.

"Stretching that metaphor with a little liberty," she began, "it will take a village to get through the climate crisis. Those amazing young women opened our hearts to a new design for our future together through collaboration. Global warming is here for the rest of our lives. We will adjust—that's called adaptation—but every community needs a continuously refined plan. Our two-county comprehensive plans need a lot more input from the citizens of our bioregion.

"Ten years ago, our non-profit worked through the counties' comprehensive plans except we included Kootenai County and all of the forested lands around Coeur d'Alene. We engaged folks from the working professions of forestry, economics, and government. Then we ventured out across the U.S. to 44 other unique counties who each took a full year to plan their climate mitigation and adaptation plans. Our approach has been methodical and scholarly and employed much less drama than these Drawdown Scholars delivered here today."

This had the flavor of a nice introductory speech and then Nancy threw her zinger. "What did these Scholars ask you to do as mayors—as city councils—and more up my alley, what are we going to do as a county? Commissioners, how will you lead our citizens into the next decade? How can we strengthen our county's comprehensive plans?"

Shelby leaned in and said, "They brought to our attention a number of policy areas for us to dive into. We needed that push. Drama can be beautiful. Who in this audience has ever heard of Rights of Nature?"

Chapter 16

GROWING PAINS AND A STONE CEREMONY

Each one of the team members wrote furiously in their journals as another group made sandwiches in the kitchen. There was not a word spoken in the living room and everyone in the kitchen also worked in silence, alone with their thoughts and feelings. Sara came to the kitchen and leaned against the door frame to admire the women working together. She cleared her throat: "We would like to begin now."

Settling around their Council Circle, Maria led by example and folded to the floor with yogini agility. Jules stayed in her chair opposite Gail. Women pulled out rolled up camp chairs or settled into supported positions on the floor. Dot arranged the Sister Scarves as an altar and passed around sticky notes. "These will help us improve."

"A sacred way to begin is through breath," Maria said. "Take in three long breaths, hold for a count of four and release, then again. Weave your breaths around the others here. One. Two. Three."

Masai had settled into a low chair with her knees up around her chin. She unwrapped her arms around her knees, folded her long legs into a beautiful lotus posture, and leaned in. She held out her hands to the women on both sides of her. One was an elder and one was younger than her granddaughters. "In gratitude, we ask Great Spirit to watch over us and guide our hearts in pure thoughts. In a moment of silence, we invite our Ancestors, too. Locate your place in the lineage of females in your families. Feel love through your left hand, your feminine side. With a squeeze send love around our circle before you release. Rest for a moment in this Council's glorious image—we have each other, always."

Jules saw that she opened her eyes before the others, so she snapped hers shut again and breathed deeply.

Gail gently emptied her four bags of Stones onto the corners of her green shawl. "This is a 20-year tradition for me. Women have probably marked Equinox for 10,000 or 30,000 years. I ask that you join me in expressing gratitude to the Ancestral Guardians of the Four Directions. Take a turn to remember the winter season just past with one sentence about your gratitude for the events of winter and place a stone in the center. After one round, we will offer another sentence for the unfolding of our prayers or intentions for spring. Sacred space is open."

While everyone remained seated, Sara rose gracefully from the floor, fluffed out her skirts and began. "We had a little meeting about this debrief with you, our whole Council. What we need from you right now is your support and suggestions on how to strengthen our presentations going forward. We've heard talk spreading about us. Our presentation at school assembly will be filmed by a documentary film producer. No one knew about the Panida until today. Forever thank you, Karen. We are scared. Are we ready for this? Speaking for myself and perhaps my teammates, I feel strong and vulnerable at the same time. Our student body needs one level of communication, but at the Panida Theater, the community requires something different. Please help us evaluate for both audiences."

Jules said, "Please put your helpful comments on a sticky note in front of us when we finish. When I journaled, I wrote about the three generations represented in this Circle. It means so much that we have your support."

They had drawn straws for their feedback. Alex drew #1 and she began. "Gail whispered that Nancy was a secret hiding in the woods. I learned about Dr. Nancy's work too late to integrate it into my presentation. I will be meeting with her separately to learn what she thinks. Her Climate Solutions University approach includes assessing risks and identifying where and how people can adapt to them.

"Vulnerable populations like the elderly, not in my inventory, need to be included in our new way of thinking. Sure, the county commissioners are supposed to do this work, but so am I. The bioregion is a commitment that I take seriously. For instance, I didn't do any comparison between urban and rural needs, but in the future, I'll dig into those details. I didn't inventory how many little watersheds we have, so that's another new learning curve for me. I love water, I learned to pray over water when I was really little and we watched Dr. Masaru Emoto's ice crystals, remember? Who knew that human consciousness has a molecular effect on water!" Throwing herself a high-five with a loud clap, she finished by exclaiming, "Our bioregion rocks!"

Alex loved to throw her fist into the air, but now she asked for feedback instead, "Please write a note to me on your sticky pads." She folded her long body onto the floor next to her enormous backpack.

Allowing long minutes for writing, to set a different example for summary thoughts, Dot said, "I drew #2 straw. Today was exactly what has kept me awake the past three days. I mostly need to stay home, walk in the woods with my little siblings and sleep. Every part of this Land Sector feels too big now. Like Alex, I can see all that I still need to do and that is exciting. I need my own dual dimensional team to continue, so in my bed at night, I imagine who I might want to have on my team: Every character from my childhood—the fairies and the tree nymphs—they feel more real than people. The ideas of how to heal different ecosystems seem to come directly from the imaginary talks I have with them."

Dot stood up and twirled around as if she was changing energies. "Did you all see how I changed energy that easily? Now I am back from dreamland and into being a Scholar again. I need someone to just tell me what's in the Comp Plan. I don't want to try and understand legal description mumbo jumbo by myself. This next need came from my research. What exactly is meant by cascading benefits? I need a team of protectors for those cascading benefits. We need to learn the value of protecting all that we have. And, I need a restoration team to help with the initial evaluations of all that has been degraded. When these two teams come together, we can create the pathways for regeneration that will actually draw down carbon. Protectors and regenerators. Where are these people? Who knows what I am even talking about? Can any of you help with these really urgent needs?" She began to cry.

Maria jumped first and wrapped Dot in her arms, "You're strong enough to cry over all that you love and all you have learned. It's a mess we can fix. I have lived here 40 years and I know people who will jump at the chance to be useful. You are still children. Probably the climate crisis is robbing you of time you could spend with your fairies and nymphs, all of you."

River joined in. "Don and I would love to be on those teams of yours." She had a heart for balance and always volunteered her husband when he was absent.

Tina added, "From what I could see when I looked at the audience, you have really rattled a lot of people. There will be resistance, but I wouldn't be surprised if people begin to line up behind the four of you. I predict that is what will happen at the Panida."

Karen laughed. "In fact, that is exactly what happened when we rolled out the Transition Town for Sandpoint. A couple of those old teams are still smoldering. People really bond over actionable steps."

Dot sucked in a deep breath. "Okay, this is how we all feel. It's temporary. We feel a little like our balloons have been popped and the wind has blown away our energy." She twisted her neck to completely release the tension and continued.

Wiping her tears on her sleeve, "Thanks for speaking about people you know, Maria. Our new task began today, and we didn't really see it coming. We woke up the adults in the village." She gave herself a high-five in the air and pointed to her team members. "In my journal, I had no critique per se. Instead, I sound lots more like my own cheerleader. I pledge to double down, to do well on my finals in my other classes and rejuvenate during spring break.

"I will really appreciate your offers, but first write a sticky note for me." After a very long pause and a drink of water, Dot sat back in the circle and nodded to Sara, "Your turn."

Bubbling over, Sara sang to a familiar melody, "Oh yay, I drew the #3 straw. What keeps me awake is the wonder of talent and gifted people who will come here for refuge. They are already coming. Personally, I would like to start up a Welcome Wagon. Which one of you told me about that? Oh Yeah, thanks J'nell." Sara gave her new friend a twinkle-eye and touched two fingers to her lips. "You probably know this, but Jules and I have created a little stream of Food-too-good-to-waste from local restaurants that's going to all the soup kitchens. Maria has already streamlined it for us. We came up with this idea hanging out with Dex twice a week while he cooked for the disadvantaged. I have learned a lot about the shadows of our community by hanging out with him those afternoons."

Sara took a long drink of water before continuing. "Seven days a week, people come to the churches around town to receive their only meal of the day. Dex told me there is a constant stream of new people. Those I've talked to are clueless and cold. They haven't researched Sandpoint very well; some can't figure out how to fit in. Maria and Dex both confirm that applications to be cooks or wait-staff are piling up at the restaurants.

"A Welcome Wagon package filled with goodies and resources would supplement my little intentional kindnesses when I serve food to them. I like it. Best part of the day, I get to eat Dex's amazing soups. When I journaled about visiting the soup kitchen just last week, I wrote, 'Seems that hunger is coming here.' I don't have time to be the watchdog for all these new people. I wonder who does? So, I want to put that into my talk. There is so much I had to leave out. My written paper is already twice as long as the assignment! And, like my teammates, I am grateful for your specific comments."

Everyone put their head down to write Sara a note. Gail wrote on a sticky note: *Your great idea for a Welcome Wagon needs to be fleshed out by the El-*

ders and delivered by them to the Chamber of Commerce.

Carefully standing up from her folding chair and twirling around, Jules sang out, "I drew #4. I would say all that time in the hospital bed preserved my energy—I feel supercharged. Instead of feeling drained, those awesome presentations filled me with energy. Also, Gail turned me on to a couple of tonic teas that help with stress. One of the most amazing is Skullcap. I have some if anyone wants a stress lift."

Gail raised her hand and jumped to her feet. "Tell me where it is? Dot needs a shot." Looking around, "You all do. I will bring you each a cup. Speak up Jules, I can hear really well."

Gail dashed into the kitchen and was back as Jules found her voice again. "I love to talk about growing food when the snow is falling. Look at those great big snowflakes." Everyone looked out and saw dollar size flakes falling slowly, like they do when the weather system stalls overhead and the wind dies down.

"My team seems to be pretty well defined—the Hope and Sandpoint Garden Club—some of you are right here. We're missing Pat Wentworth, the wonder woman. Dot's people are the only farmers among us except our heroine, Diane Green. Where is she? And how will we build bridges across the conservative bastion that dominates our communities. Can we do that without feeling awkward?"

J'nell had been quietly watching. "Progressives make progress. Gail has been gone a few seasons. We're already holding our holiday gatherings together with the Bonner County Gardeners Association and trading invitations. Of course, you remember Grey? He invited all of us to the Christmas party. It was a little awkward because we tend to be cliquish, but when I whispered in everyone's ear to adopt a new friend, we mingled and had a marvelous time. Because of our professional lives and our people skills, one-on-one brings out our shine. Honey, we are not at all awkward."

Jules took back the floor. "I have classmates who will enlist their moms and dads and grandparents." Looking around, "two of our boyfriends are cowboys and the captain of the basketball team is a grass farmer. We only know our generation but many of our classmates are the fourth generation from Sandpoint. There's a club for that."

She sat back down. "Sometimes the food sector seems like a no-brainer: Why are we food insecure with such abundance? Scholars, we have stirred the cauldron, haven't we?"

Alex wanted another turn; she felt well cheered up by her teammates. "Well, out of the mist walks Dr. Nancy." She looked around to the elders and asked, "How many of you know her personally?"

Half of the hands shot in the air. Karen said, "J'nell and I were on Nancy's board of directors a few years back."

Alex cleared her throat. "My own learning curve just went straight up and down again. This could be something to cry over or it could be the next piece of our puzzle. In the very beginning of our Project, we agreed to the boundaries of our bioregion and chose two counties instead of three. That was a lucky move. It never occurred to me to examine the Comprehensive Plans our two counties already have in place. Right after finals, I will dig into those and get to know Nancy. Dot you can't go alone to see the wizard in the woods. I'm coming too!

Sister Water Stone Spirit surprises: Can you hear her?

Radical: Resistance: Rewild: Regenerate:
Extremely Local, as in Local-Local

R'evolution, as in everything

Wake up to dream sharing and coffee
Talk until action is obvious,
Do The Work that is yours to do.
We are the Earth loving ourselves.

Chapter 17

DREAM BREAK TO THE ESCALANTE DESERT

Since the elders had made the sandwiches, the girls decided they would serve. The altar was transformed into a luncheon, the lazy Susan from the kitchen table now sat in the middle. Little sticky notes said vegan or sparse turkey. No one talked of leaving. Their debrief was over but sharing a light meal capped their energies.

Dot wanted to talk about spring break. She had the largest family and needed a few details for Dorothy and Jerry. Looking around to the elders in the circle, she asked, "Do any of you observe spring break when the schools do?"

No one had a chance to answer Dot's question, instead, an eruption: Alex had something brewing inside of her. "Every part of our grand scheme to take two vans and four families to the Utah desert is fantastical. I mean, who wouldn't drool over Dex as chef-in-residence and tour guide."

Sara bragged about her other dad until he had agreed to his assigned tasks and began the planning. That part had been fun for the girls, especially when Sara brought out the Utah topos. She voiced her wonder aloud. "Dex has been to Escalante plenty of times with his biker group. That was another life before Sandpoint, before Jon and me."

Alex had objections. Like a volcano going off, Alex was the brainiac analyst who deconstructed this business-as-usual plan. As much as it hurt her heart too, she pointed out all the parts of the proposed trip that harmed the Earth and hurt their spirits. Animated and releasing her pent-up energy, Alex enumerated: "First it's not local-local. We would spend lots of money outside our bioregion. Second, even though we could spend all our donations on carbon credits besides tons of cash on gas, this is philosophically harmful. Didn't we pledge to keep transportation local as much as possible until the transition to solar-electric cars? Isn't that why we decided we could leave the Transport Sector out of our Drawdown presentations?"

Everyone was stunned into silence. This eruption had a shadow of shaming, a lot of grief, and something else—something more like emergence—Alex needed to hear herself take a stand for the Earth. "When I dreamed last Thursday about crying all the way home from Utah, I knew I had to tell you. No. I mean, I woke up with tears, with my heart beating fast. No. I can't go. None of us can go. Not now. We are Drawdown Scholars. Dex will have to show us his slide show and we will have to break for play a different way."

After she ticked all those details off with her fingers, Alex said simply, "I've been imprinted by the community looking back at us from the audience. We've stood in front of our collective government officials and in front of middle schoolers and elders. We claimed that the pendulum is swinging the other way. We caused it to swing. The best thing we can do now is tell Ben Olson at Sandpoint Reader about this radical shift. It's our headline news."

"Bravissima!" Maria exclaimed. "Let's do that Alex. Let's create a story from what you just said and submit it to the Reader. This is wonderful drama." As light as a feather, Maria got up and folded Alex into her arms.

Jules was raking her fingers through her hair. Dot looked pasty and grief stricken. Sara needed to cry. Masai rescued everyone with a question, "What can you harvest from this explosive energy? We are learning to harvest our feelings of grief from all that we're learning at these gatherings. Just now, the Earth cracked open and gave birth to you as Eco-warriors, I mean the Goddess variety of warrior. How can you use this moment to build all of us into a fierce female force for good, for Goddess Gaia?"

Gail reached again for her sparkly bag of gemstones, those that made each altar bright and energized. Karen and J'nell had cleaned up the luncheon when no one was looking. "I have been waiting for this juicy moment, Alex. Thank you. I had no idea how or when, but I need to offer you a gift. This tiny gift comes inspired by Crazy Horse, Lakota war leader of the Oglala band of Plains Indians. A seer all his life, he was challenged when the army came after his lands and his people. A small brown stone behind his ear protected him and today the Lakota people hold their warrior legacy. They have persevered."

Shaking the bag, Gail passed it around and said, "Moon-wise. We go with the Moon because she is the old Grandmother of the Earth. Peek inside and take a stone from this bag and ask it what you feel from all this emotional energy, what emotion will serve you in the days and weeks ahead? Drop it in your pocket and check with yourself often; *how is my emotional intelligence*?"

At the end of their debrief, a quick group hug and congratulations dispersed everyone due to the winter storm warning that kept buzzing their cellphones. From mid-January, the county sheriff alerts had not slowed down. 2020 was a snowy winter.

Dot was spending the night with Sara who had a convenient extra bed-room. They invited all the parents but didn't expect many to show up. It continued to snow through the afternoon. Texts around to everyone said the Escalante camping trip needed to be cancelled. Not a lot of explanation, the 6 p.m. meet-up time and address were included. Slide show of Escalante was highlighted. Bring pizza, please. The girls had spent an hour of the afternoon in a nap puddle on Jules' bed. Then they suited up to get over to Sara's for the slide show. They walked very slowly and held Jules steady.

Cancelling their dream trip to Escalante had brought an eco-storm of emo-tions. Probably they needed their little gemstones to remind them to check-in. Sitting around Sara's plush living room with a big screen TV, Jules wondered aloud, "Why haven't we been over here before?"

Sara blushed and stammered, "Because the boys are so private and you were in a hospital bed—two reasons why, I guess. I convinced Dex to show us what we're missing by not going to Utah. Dex is coming out in another way and sharing his living room. It's his idea. Sara cried over the phone when she told him why. "Mostly, it would be five or six days of driving and we would be away for the Rights of Nature Declaration Ceremony."

This was another clincher. The tribes had a strong response to the Scholars presentation to the government. A Tribal Elder had escorted Jane Fritz to the Event Center and wanted to respond in kind. They planned on a City Beach Ceremony to honor the lake and invited all the tribal peoples who had strong unwritten laws about the Rights of Nature.

Dot protested. "Driving is what spring break used to be all about. We al-ways looked forward to the whole family being together, sleeping and singing all the way to somewhere and all the way back. It's very hard to be an Eco-war-rior all the time."

Jules trying to be bright. "I still need to use my season pass at Schweitzer since the doc cleared me to ski the bunny hill. After 90 days of healing, I've been ordered not to fall." They had made the decision together. After Alex's speech, how could they go? They all agreed to compromise. In this spirit of cooperation and compromise, they shifted rather easily by putting their hands into their center pile and throwing yeses into the air. "For the Earth," they shouted. They sealed their own energy shift, but they still had to explain to their families. Their decision affected the vacations of 15 other individuals.

Around the fire, they played charades. Sam joined them for pizza and the Escalante slide show; she stayed because her parents stayed. Even though finals week started Monday, this was no time to cram.

Everyone kissed and hugged, and the girls fell into their deep sleeps. When they woke in the morning, they were Eco-warriors who still had a week of finals ahead. The group had the benefit of divine invitations from Maria and Masai for several sessions of art therapy in the tipi. Everyone tried hard to be happy they were not going to the desert rocks of southern Utah. Through the arc of childhood behind them, they could barely see the trajectory ahead. Maria advised that as they grew into womanhood, working with the contrast of their inner child would help them see the next version of themselves more clearly.

Jules made two short trips to the ski-hill. Alex usually skied all day, but Jules had ventured up there with her friend and returned bored with the bunny hill. Besides, tightening a ski boot around her wound hurt too much. Sara was not all that fond of skiing and Dot showed up a couple of times to cross-country. She never missed one of the free days.

Gail had not planned on going to southern Utah for all the reasons Alex and the others endorsed. In fact, she disappeared after the debrief luncheon and the girls didn't know when they would see her again. Twenty hungry people who had originally planned to go to Escalante met at Jalapenos' Restaurant on the third night of spring break to see how they were handling the shift to being Eco-warriors. Parents and siblings had been casualties of an energy they didn't fully understand.

Alex stood at the head of the long table in the private dining room and tapped her spoon on her glass. Kids continued to chow down on tortilla chips and guacamole but looked at her with as much attention as they could spare. "The unanimous decision to cancel our long-planned camping trip affected each of you and we are sorry that we dragged you into our fantasy dream trip as long as we did. The other night Dex showed us a slide show and it's true, we are missing awesome rock vistas and secret hiding places in the desert. This feels right. We are closer as a community by staying right here in our bioregion.

The girls' moms shifted next and planned a short outing to Hot Springs. They would stay three nights in one of the cabin-tents, mothers on the beds and girls on their pads. Yes, it would be a chilly 30° at night and 50° in the day, but hot water heated the tents so everyone would be super comfortable.

Dorothy spoke up. "Besides, the desert in the winter is unpredictable. If the temp went below 30°, we would not have hot water in our tents to warm us up." At the Hot Springs they would soak their worries away in the glorious thermal water.

Even though they all knew the Nori carbon credits lasted forever, the group unanimously decided Jon would use them to go to Robert McKee's Screenwriter's Class. The credits would balance the flight emissions. It had happened innocently enough, Jon confessed. "After Christmas I began journaling about Sara's excitement around the Drawdown book. When I went online to have a look for myself, I ordered ten books and kept journaling. For a very long time I have wanted to be a screenwriter.

"My journaling took on mythic qualities, like a Hero's journey. When I filled one notebook and reached for a second one, I decided to take a leap. Sara and her teammates have been good subject matter; their story has the bones of a real drama with local characters. The girls play themselves, of course. Viggo Mortensen could play my character. I applied to the Screencraft Writers' Conference April 24 to 27 in Chicago. It costs $575, so the Nori credits will help a lot—I am committed. It's coming up soon; I am grateful and excited that you all want to help."

"Every part of this Drawdown story will be included," Dex said. "Especially, Rights of Nature. After break, we will all feel the drumbeat building up to the dramatic and personal story at the Panida on May 15—it's not so far away."

Plans were finalized for the Hot Springs trip. Jon and Dex both wanted to go but it was decided it would be an all-woman trip. They were cool with that since they have a hot tub anyway. The younger kids were also invited. Dot suggested, "We could tell animal encounter stories. Everyone can bring stories about their favorite thrilling or scary wildlife adventures."

Alex's brother Paul perked up, "Yeah, do they scare you or thrill you? I want to hear about the scary ones."

Dot answered in her firm voice. "Gail told us about laying down off-trail while a bear turned and went the other way. To me that seemed really scary. I have always been thrilled to encounter a wild animal. What I noticed being a country girl, is you guys want to talk about your favorite movies with fake animals. I hardly even know what you're talking about. Bring real stories, okay?"

Their conversation at Jalapeno's was interrupted by a flash blizzard. While they were putting on their winter gear, Robin spoke up in defense of animated movies. "We always thought the value lessons were good from some of those movies. Lots of them jerked pretty hard on our hearts. But I would drive to work wondering if last night's movie helped shape my girls in any good way. I noticed how different they responded when the animals and the characters were real."

"I often wondered why the movie studios didn't give those animated parts to real actors and actresses," Jon said. "Sure, the animation artists have a good gig in Hollywood, but real people need work and our children need to be entertained by something deeper than fantasy fiction."

The two seniors spoke up. This was their last ever spring break; they were sulky and silent. They had been accepted to the University of Idaho and Evergreen State and were headed for Washington together. Jules' older sister Sam was more vocal than Alex's brother. They were an item and held hands under the table. Sam raised their hands to show everyone their intertwined fingers. "We definitely would not smother our kids with those movies."

Paul barely said anything. "Yeah, I vote for more nature, too." Lately, he had struggled with his parent's divorce and lived in a townhouse with four other seniors who wanted to experience living on their own before college.

"Could you tell me bear stories?" Dot's little sister asked. "That's what I want. I don't want to wait for the trip to Hot Springs."

Chapter 18

FEARLESS LIKE A MOUNTAIN LION

The trip required two big SUVs to transport the crowd over to Hot Springs, Montana but the drive took only three hours rather than three days. When they circled up in the shallow end of the thermal pool, there were thirteen heads bobbing and swooning over the water.

"Think of the origin of this amazing gift," Jules said softly. She closed her eyes, the air was crisp and the water hot, she wiggled her toes.

Catching the drift of Jules' thought, Dot mused, "I wonder how deep under Earth's mantle the source of this water is.

So, this was their spring break. April had sneaked up on them. On the drive over they noticed less and less snow covering the ground. A different ecosystem surrounded the valley around Hot Springs where the Thompson River flows.

When they finally emerged, gloriously wrinkled from hot pools, Sara said, "I am really liking the silence—I've talked more in February and March than ever in my life! You know, the animal encounter I still remember is our ermine. It's still a strong image."

"Tell me more," Robin said, acting as Sara's substitute mother, because Dex had stayed behind. He had done his level best to be Sara's adopted mother; he often reminded her how he changed her diapers and tended her through childhood measles. When he stayed behind, he told Sara that he wasn't really looking forward to the long drive to southern Utah anyway. But it was hard to not join the mothers on this trip. He knew she would be well taken care of by her best friends.

Looking around the table inside the Symes rustic restaurant, Sara locked eyes with a curious girl across the table. Even though she knew Dot's sister had more wildlife stories than she did, she asked her, "Have you ever seen an ermine in the winter? I had never seen one before and I couldn't imagine, so, try to imagine." She held her hands over her dinner dish and cupped them together. "I think she could curl up in my two hands." Then Sara used two fingers to stroke the imagined fur. "From her nose to her tail, maybe she was 12 inches."

Sara flashed a twinkle eye across the table to Sam. So began a long night of tales about wild sightings. Everybody had stories, some quite exotic. When

Alex's mother finally spoke, everyone turned to her because she had hardly said a word. "I've got one that Alex hasn't heard. We can go into dreamtime with this story." Secretly Deborah was happy to tell the last tale and find the silence before dreams came.

"We still lived way up the Pack. I had been to town, Alex, you were about seven, I think. I'd had lunch with a long-lost friend and her daughter, so my thoughts were on that happy reunion. I rounded the corner before the Pack River bridge, about six miles up the canyon, and a cougar dropped off the steep side of the hill and crossed the road. She was so sleek and big—I lightly tapped my brakes—but she was swift. From nose to tail, her body occupied both lanes of the road.

"At the end of the first week in January, the snow was fluffy; the mid-January rains had not come yet. Cougar dropped off the edge where there was a bit of space, a frozen wetland that edged the River. I continued to slow down until I stopped at the trail she had made. She was down there with an elk carcass. For some reason, I leaned forward to look up the hill where she came from and realized she had made a deep trail between the carcass and her den—I knew she had a litter of kittens up there.

"Up the canyon we had a phone tree, you know to keep track of each other up and down the Pack. I checked around with two of my friends: Jane had also seen Cougar, and Tosha had the most incredible news. I asked her if she was keeping it to herself. She said no, check your answering machine. Sure enough, it was blinking. Tosha said she was coming down the canyon to work at the Samuels Store when she saw the cougar attached to an elk's neck cross the road in front of her—scared her half out of her mind. She almost had an accident; she was still quivering."

Alex fell asleep with her mother's bedtime tale. When they all woke in the morning the stories continued. When she stretched herself out of her sleeping bag, thrilled to be warm in the sheep-herder's style tent Alex asked, "Anyone for snowshoeing?" As she laced up her boots no one even moved. She wiggled her fingers and quickly passed through the flap, closing it down behind her.

Pink alpenglow hung on the ridges. This was Alex's private secret, get out there while the critters were waking up. Maybe they were heading for bed. Only one trail led up and away from Symes Resort. The snow had not been deep, the trail was packed. She probably didn't need snowshoes, but a packed trail was not her destination. She spotted a stone outcropping and headed for it.

Quieting her mind, she remembered her mother's story of the night before. Closing her eyes, she envisioned the face of Cougar, including her long whiskers.

Alex realized this was her animal ally now. She kept her eyes closed, hoping the image would linger. Her eyes sprung open, she thought she saw a cougar off in the distance as it disappeared into the trees. She asked, "How can I serve you Mother Cougar?"

That question would stay with Alex for a decade. How would it fit into the mission of her presentation about the bioregion? How can I serve? This was the philosophical question their Godmother Dolores asked. When she put it all together, Alex realized her personal task would be to recover and preserve the wild places in her bioregion—this was her commitment. How could she even leave for college? Everything she needed was right here, with her father and her mysterious mother, with her younger sister and brother. So much happened in those nanoseconds, Alex felt like she had crossed into magical energy through the wrinkle of time. When she wiggled her fingers and toes, she came back into her body. Once again she wanted to be an accredited ecologist.

She climbed down off her rock and headed back toward the trail. Moving slowly, Alex realized deep tracks led away from the big rock face. When she looked straight down on them, she saw Cougar had been right there, she knew it. Now she had her own cougar story.

Back at the resort, Alex wanted to soak and sit with her morning experience. Her teammates were already in the pool, waving at her; they had left their sleeping bags and gone straight to the water. She held her story inside; it was a vision for the future.

Dot said almost nothing the whole day. She was puzzling over a cinematic dream. Parts of it were apocalyptic and parts were like Heaven on Earth. The energy of it felt like a Yo-Yo, pushing and pulling with equal force. What was she supposed to do with those clear images? After she soaked, she wrote the whole thing down in her journal. As she was journaling, Jules asked, "Did you dream last night?"

Dot nodded. "Yeah. Did you?"

"I dreamed so many animals, like a parade, and at the end they were all locked in a zoo. I woke up terrified for them. I decided it was a message—I need to become a defender of wildlife."

The second morning, Sara stayed last in her sleeping bag. When she finally got up, she asked, "Did any of you sleep?" When she realized she was the only one who was sleepless for most of the night, she confessed to being challenged by all those animal stories. "You know, I'm a city girl at heart. I puzzled a long time over all those stories we have been sharing." She summarized, "I started it with the ermine, but think about it: three bear sightings, a pair of baby eaglets, touching the gigantic antlers of a bull elk, lots of moose sightings in town, two different cougars, one wolf, lots of coyotes, and a beautiful little bobcat. I couldn't stop their messages from streaming through my mind and challenging me to stand up for their rights."

BEING SEEN

Make no mistake, the Earth's eye has been watching.
It holds our collective consciousness.
Rarely do we think of stones as Ancestors, but here is your invitation.

What is the collective consciousness of today?
Have not the children brought Climate Justice into the hearts and minds of billions?

When the Twin Towers went down, we were so distracted.
Now they say, that happened before I was born.
Earth is what I care about, not war.

This eye of the Earth reflects back only darkness, no humor, no promises. She draws us into unfathomable depths. The kids see this: It's time for all to see.

Answering Earth's Call   133

Chapter 19

ONE LAST TANGO

On the first of May they were supposed to mail their final written papers to Gail. The team members had returned from break with something like a spiritual mission, but they hadn't talked much.

When they did all gather in the tipi for *#FridaysforFuture* time with their fellow protesters, the conversations included the work of teens from around the world, like the Sunrise Movement and the Extinction Rebellion. With J'nell's help, local teens were discovering interbeing—a state of connectedness—and faith. Somehow, they had discovered each other. New strengths arose from sitting with the elders and others in the quiet of their Council Circles. A regular Circle sprung up spontaneously in the basement of the Gardenia Center after Sunday service.

Gail called a meeting of Consultants and asked the Scholars to come. They set aside two hours after lunch. "What has changed for you this month?" Gail asked. They realized something had happened to them while they soaked in the Earth's healing waters over spring break. What had changed, they were not sure until Gail showed them the thread back to it. "You have all doubled your efforts."

Dot wiggled in her chair. "I've searched for the exact moment when things changed for me and my April 1st journal entry reminded me of the first night at the Hot Springs. We told lots of animal stories to fall asleep. It was a half Moon in Cancer." Dot continued. "I've enjoyed tracking Grandmother Moon and my personal Moon-time. Isn't Cancer the sign of home?"

Her teammates were flipping through their journals. "OMG. Fuck," Alex blurted. "It was April Fool's Day! I had a vision that morning: Cougar was the messenger. She asked for a commitment from me while I sat on a rock outcropping. I gave her my whole heart." She looked around to the others and completed her thought, "Remember my mother's cougar story?"

Jules said rather sadly, "Yeah, my dream haunts me. A long line of animals trailed across my field of vision and ended up in zoo pens. It was awful. I will tell you what cheers me up. At one of our early meetings Gail gave us a handout called *Entelechy*. Remember it? She asked us to evolve the word independent. A light bulb when off when J'nell taught us about interbeing. This is interdependence that Gail referred to. We are related to the wild and we need each one of those critters so we can know ourselves."

Sara stared at Jules and could not believe her ears. "That is so weird! Listen to what I wrote that day: April 1. Couldn't sleep. Felt haunted by all those animal stories. When I finally slept, I was counting animals, two cougars, three bears, a pair of eaglets, one wolf, two coyotes. She snapped her journal closed and said, "OMG! What did you say about a Cancer Moon? Did we all dream about the same animals? We are interbeing with them!"

Reaching out her hands to form a connection to each one of these visionaries, Gail asked, "What are we doing all this work for? Who? Why?"

Silence held them all together. Laura Adams, their vivacious mentor and sometimes shrink, found them at the back table. "Something just happened," she said. "I can feel it."

"I think they all discovered Rights of Nature by some miracle of the Moon and the Hot Springs over break," Gail explained. She made eye contact with Laura and deeper messages were exchanged. "The Scholars just discovered they all were visited by the same wild animals in their dreams. Some energy was deeply mysterious, some of it was frightening, all of it was sacred." Looking adoringly at her Scholars, Gail explained to Laura, "They have all released their academic papers to me, so we gathered here to celebrate. I could sense a dramatic change. I asked a couple of questions, like why are we doing this work. Now their group visionary experiences just added a whole new dimension."

Sara wrapped up their thoughts and feelings for Laura who had taught them to use emotions in their pursuit of knowledge. "Each one of us independently received the answer from dreamtime a month ago: It's for the sacred Others we are doing this work. If they have a protected place here in the bioregion, so do we."

Laura beamed, "Okay then. Let's celebrate."

As the other tables filled up with Consultants, Jules felt a speech rising in her. She asked Sara if she could go first. Tapping a spoon against the glass, she said, "Good to see all of you in one place. I'm standing up for the animals today and announcing we're ready for the Panida even though none of us knew that until five minutes ago. I feel great awe and gratitude for Karen and her gang for making such a big stir over our event two weeks from now. Yikes!"

Jules stood up to talk. "Over spring break, we were all visited by animal spirits from real-life wild sightings that filled our storytelling time. Privately, we dug into our work with the powerful motivation to serve the animals of the Earth, and Great Mother herself. We didn't know we had all received the same animal visitations until just a couple of minutes ago. Speaking for myself, I am ready to stand up and speak up. A haunting dream of the last animals on Earth parading into zoos will guide me forever."

She motioned to Sara who stood up. "I am working for wildlife and I've decided to do it through the fashion industry." Stirrings and whispered comments followed her declaration. "I know. I know." She motioned with her hands to quiet the confusion. "When I returned from break, I watched a couple of fast fashion documentaries that made me sit straight up and examine my clothes closet with clear eyes.

"Do you realize the negative environmental impact of fast fashion? Water pollution, toxic chemicals and textile waste, to name a few. Before the end of the second movie, I promised the Earth I would change. If I can change, we can all change." She felt like she had lots more to say, but the women in the room had stood and were applauding. Sara loved the irony in her chosen Sector, Materials.

Alex jumped right out of her chair. "Sounds like my Solutions Sector is going to do very well in this audience. Right-on for you, Sara. Women and Girls will rise in service to the Earth. I've been watching the Moon too. That single journal entry on April 1st under the Cancer Moon changed my whole focus. After college I am looking forward to supporting women entrepreneurs right here in our bioregion and taking pre-teen girls into the woods in search of wild animal signs and to learn about the Rights of Nature. I need to gather the skills as an educator, first."

Dot grabbed her red hair into a twist. "I'm so glad to hear about your revelations. You know the rockslide kept me out of school for a week, so I wrote and read and wrote some more—deep immersion. My dreamtimes stare back at me from the realm of choices. Either we are going to be caught in a total apocalypse or the Earth's people will realize her quivering, her earthquakes, volcanoes and viruses are her way of sending a message.

"Mother Earth has been plodding through evolution to create conditions for Creator to bring about awesome variations of birds and plants, of animals and fish. I mean who can't see God and Goddess working together everywhere we look? Can someone explain the reason moose have paddles for antlers and elk can scratch butts with theirs? I have wondered about this for years and years. So, yeah. I still want to go to Evergreen State to study wildlife ecology, but I'll be here every summer. Sisters! Your visions are awesome!"

"Enjoy your lunches. I have picked up the tab already, sorry to run." Gail headed for the bathroom and kept on going. Secretly she was working on the brochure for the Panida. Several of her Consultants were in on the scheme to bring the rural model front and center to match the girls' presentations.

Gail emailed the girls: *Sorry to leave abruptly. I'm on deadline. Will explain later. Please remind the Consultants, we meet one more time before your presentations for our Gratitude Circle in the tipi, May 8, snacks and ceremony and final logistics. I've dedicated this time for your final papers. Great work all of you!*

Standing up after lunch, catching the energies gathering around the teenagers, Karen said, "It's been a long time since I had this much fun. We divvied up the tasks of our Drawdown Scholars Presentation in two weeks. I've sent all of you a PDF of the program. Please look at it carefully and send me any corrections. We pulled in Cindy Peer due to threats made on our Facebook page. There may be counter-protests around gun ownership and abortion rights. We've stirred up the whole cauldron here. Cindy will coordinate with the local police and the sheriff's office. We're not yet certain if they are the protestors they pretend to be—Cindy has already butted heads with a female deputy, even though no one lives who is gentler or more diplomatic than our Cindy.

"Angels Over Sandpoint will make our goodies and offer a bake sale and half the proceeds will go to feed the children, our pet project." She stood behind Gaea and rested her hand on one shoulder. "Just so you know, SuZen will handle lighting in the theater and watch for projector problems on the PowerPoint. Jane will bring two Chiefs for opening prayers. Tina has graciously agreed to be our Master of Ceremonies.

"The Consultants will pass our bowls for donations for the teens and for the brochure printing costs to repay Gail." Then she put her hand over her mouth and said, "Oops, I am supposed to keep that secret. Gail is working with Diane on the rural manual outlining how Drawdown and the Sectors work especially well in rural communities." She laughed her most infectious laugh. Her arm shot skyward, index pointing, "Ready, set, go. See you in the tipi next Friday. What time?"

At 1:00 pm the following Friday, Gail bowed at the entrance of the tipi. Wafting the smudge smoke that engulfed her, she looked around and realized she had not been in the tipi for well over a month. Justin jumped up and unfolded a camp chair, "Which direction today, Grandmother? North?" Gail nodded. Then she placed her bags and sticks in the chair and kneeled in front of it to set a new altar.

After she laid out the shawl and her direction sticks, she placed the bags of Stones in the corners of the cloth and took her chair, closing her eyes. The news of resistance had been alarming yet Gail wondered why she was surprised. In 2016, white supremacy had been given new life in North Idaho.

Women from the inner circle around the Scholars sent out invitations to the event via their network of Facebook friends and then secretly advised each other to stay off social media. By email, the word about discord circulated—no one should add fuel to the fire. But the threats mounted.

Cindy watched anonymously from her secret identity. She talked daily to her friend at the Bonner County Sheriff's office. Terry Horton agreed that the threats were serious, and she worked overtime following those leads. About to retire, Terry remembered the standoff at Ruby Ridge and how intimidated her younger self had felt by threats that most citizens had not even known about. The State Police took cyber-threats very seriously, but especially the death threats.

When Gail opened her eyes again, tears had welled up and spilled over onto her old and wrinkled cheeks. When she pulled out a red handkerchief, she realized everyone was watching her. "We have all been psychologically learning to process with our dear friend, Laura. Together and separately she's leading us through grief. Now we will use intention and prayer—whichever works best for you—to spin a cloak of protection around all our Earth-friendly activities. What we have recently witnessed from both ends of the bioregion, up and down the watersheds, is raw fear cracking open. The extra alerts will ensure our safety and we already know that evil will not win out. This dark underbelly needs some air and lots of love. Are we clear? We are the ones who bring joy.

"Who wants to lead this ceremony?"

All four Scholars raised their hands. They had slept over at Sara's and dressed up for this day with just the right amount of bling, blush, and mascara; they were made for this work.

Alex began. "Ceremony comes like a teaching from Mother Spider. We have learned that we can go to the church of choice on Sunday with our families, because one level of comfort has always come from that community. Then we enter this TipiTemple on Friday—or any other day—and feel connected to the whole planet, to the animal spirits, and to each other." Fifteen teens sat shoulder to shoulder in the south direction, feeling clear and comfortable. Alex smiled at the clarity of her little speech and looked at Jules to go next.

Speaking without hesitation, "Guardians of the Four Directions, we stand before you with prayers of gratitude today, casting off our fears, our doubts, and transforming the criticism of those still in the dark."

Sara spoke up next feeling especially vulnerable. "Ancestors, I give thanks for my diversity and I ask for extra love that my teammates are safe being around me. Oh, God!" She had not known those words were even there but she understood her privilege more each day.

Dot was firm in her voice. "It is our clear intention that safety will prevail, and love will win. I give thanks for all the critters. Let's go around and speak the name of one we feel unity with—Deer."

"Wolf. Dog. Cat. Eagle. Owl. Grizzly. Beaver. Otter. Goat. Cow. Horse. Elk. Salmon. Trout. Wolverine. Badger." The kids increased the energy with their popcorn voices. A few pets were thrown in and several 4-H projects. Their sound crescendo for critters resembled a pep rally.

Now, lowered to gentle whispers, the elders around the outside added their voices: "Frog. Snake. Bluebird. Hawk. Lion. Earthworm. Geese. HoneyBee." Hattie had come last and was glad to be heard.

Gail from Spokane stood where her granddaughter sat cross-legged, Lena, very shy and gifted. She spoke last. "For Gaia, our Earth Mother, we feel the wound of industrialization. Standing up in this way, we strengthen hope that this work is ours to do. Civilization may be crumbling all around us, but here in our communities love is growing stronger along the silken threads of Mother Spider."

Maria gave last minute instructions. "We are now going to walk two blocks to the theater. The police have formed a barricaded path for us to enter the front doors. You Consultants are everywhere watching. Your grounding cords connect to the center of the Earth and reach to the Moon. We will be safe."

Chapter 20

RESISTANCE REFLECTS SHADOW AND LIGHT

The front spread and the inside fold of the Sandpoint Reader raised the community interest to a new level. The printed version offered the Panida Program details and the second printing flew off the stands. The website received hundreds of hits overnight. Mason had received an invitation from Gail but she didn't need an excuse to visit her hometown.

"This might be interesting," Mason sent via text. *"See ya there."* Gail knew Mason's mom and sister were coming to open their lake-front house for the summer. It was a no-brainer. Mason thought she might even get material for one of her non-college writing assignments. She enjoyed writing under a pseudonym for the Reader. Ben Olson was the only person who knew the identity of YoSerious Graduate; he supported her dream of practicing radical and thoughtful eco-journalism.

Putting their efforts where they thought it might payoff, the Reader rolled movie cameras down the aisles and parked them in prime locations five rows back from the stage and off to both sides in the wing seats.

When the Facebook Event Invite grew hostile, Gail alerted the Consultants. "This is a flashing red flag," she wrote on the email screen-shot of death threats. J'nell talked to Cindy who talked to Terry at the Bonner County Sheriff's office who contacted the Idaho State Patrol. The phone tree just yesterday had taken less than 30 minutes. In North Idaho, where reputed white supremacists hide in the woods, threats are not common because the FBI has been watching for decades. When they were alerted, someone in the office searched the IP addresses. Four agents and two canines boarded a jet from Seattle to Sandpoint. The escalation had warranted this response. They were in the air when the teens entered the tipi. Sandpoint airport is small, but it does support eight-seater jets.

County Sheriff vehicles with their lights flashing blocked off the lower parking lot behind the Panida sign that read, "Participant Passes Only" and diverted quite a few people who went on down to City Beach to gather in protest. Those folks had walked into a Sheriff's surveillance trap with only one choice, to keep on walking. "Be peaceful and sit down for a couple of hours," the deputies told the crowd. Officially identified as resisters, they were told they had to wait to re-cross the bridge over Sand Creek.

Effectively, this cut the crowd of resisters in half. Terry had proposed this idea and was surprised to hear on her radio that it seemed to be working.

Gail held Maria's hand on her left and Hattie's on her right. The Consultants formed a shield around the four teens and fearlessly they walked the short distance to the front of the Panida Theater. Sheriffs knew of this approach and created a clear path. The shouts were deafening: "First Amendment!" and "Baby killers!" Any excuse to throw those barbs, Gail thought. It had nothing to do with global warming.

This front door approach meant the tipi crowd would walk the aisles of the theater. This was all part of the plan. They did one last cheer in the lobby and split into two groups. Consultants had saved the front row seats for them which was brilliant because the theater was packed.

When Jane Fritz spoke her short introduction, the Kootenai Chief stepped forward with an arm gently placed on the shoulder of a young woman. Together they accepted a standing ovation and the younger woman spoke. "We thank you all. The Kootenai, the Kalispel, and the Nimiipuu of this region have worked mighty hard to reach the place where you would cheer any one of us. I accept your applause on behalf of the Ancestors and the Unborn Generations.

"I am One in a lineage of First People who travels back 13,000 years right here in this place." She wore a traditional gown with decorative sleeves that exaggerated her gestures and seemed to circle the whole audience. She spoke a blessing in her native language, preserved for the Nez Perce people through persistent efforts by Tribal Elders.

Sitting on the front row, the Scholars grasped each other's hands and listened until she finished and the applause stopped. Dot whispered, "Showtime." They stepped forward to go up the left stairs together. Left offers feminine power. They planned to descend the right stairs for balance.

Nothing ever goes perfectly according to plan. SuZ was set up in the middle, guarding the PowerPoint and someone threw a coke at her that splashed all over the AV equipment. Everyone saw the act and the perpetrator was immediately removed.

"We are blessed with very thoughtful and experienced Consultants," Sara said confidently. "While we wait for our backup equipment, we ask for your watchful eyes to prevent a reoccurrence. I have lived here since I was a tiny baby, and ya know, I'm not surprised at this resistance showing up. Can you imagine being one of the few people of color in the whole town? Well yeah, my dads were both feeling crazy-brave the day they decided to go all out and adopt me."

Jules accepted the mic from Sara and said, "You are crazy-brave every day of your life, Sara. I will introduce my teammates while we wait for our first slide." Jules had opted to sit down in her wheelchair after she climbed up the stairs on her own power. She rolled up to the edge of the stage, "We recognize opposition to change. The resisters are not even opposing us, they are opposing their own opening. We recognize the cauldron of issues for this time, mid-2020. The whole decade ahead will be needed to unravel all of the issues and reweave them for the Earth and her species. Today, we focus our efforts on reversing global warming. Maybe that will help with the other issues.

"We call ourselves Drawdown Scholars." She ticked off her fingers to explain STEM. "Science. Technology. Engineering. Math. Ordinarily STEM doesn't cause such a stir. Standing with us we have a planet of protesting teenagers, thanks to *#FridaysforFuture* and our heroine, Greta Thunberg. Thanks also to the Sunrise Movement and Extinction Rebellion. Around us, locally, we have been adopted by an amazing Circle of Consultants." They sat strategically all around the theater. "Will you wave, please?"

Jules pointed toward her sparkly friend Dot who chose lots of bling for this day. "Dot Moore represents the Wilderness for us. She hails from Flume Creek and you're lucky if you know where that is. Alex Olson will wrap it up by talking about entrepreneurial opportunities for everyone here. She grew up way up the Pack River, so she's our mountain girl. I'm Jules Pergosi. I was born in Selle Valley, grew up growing food as a little girl and I still love growing food. Now, I love living in town with most of you.

"I'm getting a signal from SuZ so the show must go on." The screen lit up her whole body and she felt fortunate that Alex had dragged her chair backwards away from the edge.

"Leading our team is Sara Best-Jewell." Returning to their rehearsed program, Sara stepped forward. "With my happy heart, I have the mission to introduce you to Drawdown." When a picture of the book, *Drawdown: The Most Comprehensive Plan Ever Proposed to Reverse Global Warming*, appeared large and bold, Sara remembered every line she'd practiced. "We're gathered today to talk about global warming.

"Remember this number—195. That's the number of nations who signed the Paris Agreement of 2016 to hold global warming to 1.5°C (centigrade). Just a reminder, that's 2.7° Fahrenheit. 195 nations actually agreed. You know, people often lack basic understanding as to what we're talking about—carbon dioxide is not the enemy, greenhouse gases are not bad, we need them to survive. If we didn't have greenhouse gases keeping the planet warm, we'd all be freezing.

"We are sad to tell you that the warming of the planet is accelerating because the layer of greenhouse gasses keeps growing thicker. It's now trapping heat from every tailpipe and every smokestack. Mother Ocean found her limit, she has absorbed as much CO_2 as she can hold. In the past four years, hundreds of places on Earth have already surpassed 3.6F° which is 2° C, well above the limit 195 nations agreed upon. Parts of Alaska and the Arctic were more than 6° F hotter in 2019. We have no time to lose."

Sara clicked on the slide that showed all the Solutions by Sector. "The original team of Drawdown Scholars mathematically determined 100 Solutions to our climate problem. For more than two years a group of writers, scientists, mathematicians, and academic advisors gathered to look for what was already pulling carbon from the atmosphere or what worked to bring it back to Earth. They found Solutions, hundreds of them, but none of them were very efficient or well known, except the forests of the planet.

"The stories inside this book are exciting, even fantastic." She clicked on their favorite, that first photo showing a winter scene and a herder on the back of a reindeer at the far edge of an enormous herd. "We started here when we were signing Jules' plaster cast the first week in January. Some Solutions like this one, called Repopulating the Mammoth Steppe require a stretch of our imaginations, because they don't really fit into our bioregion. Drawdown writers and scholars examined each Solution by history, its impact of carbon moving in both directions, with a story about how the solution works. Carbon continuously moves, combining with other elements, mostly with oxygen to go up into the atmosphere and come back down.

"This slide with 100 Solutions shows the hard work of the original Drawdown Scholars: We found our 17 Solutions through common sense." Sara turned sideways rustling her full skirts to look at the screen. "We listed them in your program for you to examine at home. Without worrying about rank or gigatons of carbon (GtC), because the scientists and mathematicians did that for us, we found these Solutions working right here in our bioregion. This is not controversial, it's sensible."

Sara was happy to surrender the mic and clicker to Alex. "We're just defining terms now. What do we mean by bioregion?" Alex clicked away from the 17 Solutions to the topo map of Boundary and Bonner Counties.

"Border-to-border, top-to-bottom, this bioregion is the totality of our two counties. We call this the chimney of Idaho—3,197 square miles, 2,046,080 acres of land. Every lake, river, every mountain is here, the unusual combination of features that define our bioregion. We claim each microclimate and each ecosystem as ours, collectively. It's likely this combination of wild and domestic make us who we are, the people of North Idaho."

"Most of you in this theater live somewhere in this bioregion. Yes, it's defined by state boundaries but also naturally defined with a dozen different watersheds, our two mountain ranges, and countless unique places that biologists call ecosystems."

Dot accepted the mic from Alex. "Why are we really here? As science students we've felt excited that people could learn from our presentations. Last week we presented to the Sandpoint High School student body, before that to the combined mayors' councils from our eight townships. In order to preserve the quality of life and save the animals that we all secretly hope to see, the four of us have spent hundreds of hours with these five areas of inquiry and four Sectors." The slide showed the original Sector diagram that the Scholars worked up in January.

Having learned so much about the simple focus of attention, Dot wanted everyone to hear her next line, so she paused and allowed tension to build through a moment of silence. "We came here today to ask for help." She clicked to the large circle of 100 Solutions from the Drawdown website. "This looks too complicated." Then she clicked back to their distilled version. "Over the past five months, our Drawdown team searched both counties for Solutions. We learned one important lesson: When elders and teens work together, our combined common sense designed, and will continue to refine, this simplified plan for our bioregion.

"We're asking for cooperation among people." Dot had worked with SuZ to key the lights. "Raise your hand if you know about one of these Solutions. Now raise your hand if you're related to people with their hands raised. Look around. This is where we begin. We are one blended community—unity comes through our relationships. Help us find the cascading benefits of these Solutions. That will strengthen our communities. Here's Jules to start us off with the Food Sector."

Chapter 21

THE WORK

Jules accepted Alex's strong arm to stand up for her presentation. When she first clicked the slide button, a beautiful white ermine filled the screen. "We started our Project here, on the Schweitzer quad. This next slide we created for the local government," she began. "It shows the eight townships designated in the bioregion. There are actually more—we left out Moyie Springs and Naples. People live all over the place; we are all equally important."

She had borrowed one of Gail's photos from Mexico, tomatoes spread out on the ground, drying. Then she clicked on the Drawdown photo from the website. "I call this *The Work*." A slide showed *The Work* above the words Resilient and Life Saving. Then she went to the slide called Food Sector to show the whole list to this audience.

"*The Work,* building community through Solutions, will be life saving for babies." The next slide was wild animal babies: fawns, chicks, humans, and teeny fishes. "We have not labored the subject of climate change, but rather the actions we can do together. These are the Solutions we have power over right here. Resilience is what we owe to one another to call ourselves community members. Our anxiety will decrease when our actions increase.

"We have all posted our academic papers. You can find them at Sandpoint Reader online. I will talk about only two Solutions here today. In the process of celebrating our rich abundance of food, Food Waste is ranked third among the leading causes of global warming—take that in for a moment. I asked for help from our two Extension Agents, Kate from Boundary and Jennifer from Bonner County—thanks for being here ladies.

"We examined the entire food system in our bioregion. We are food insecure because trucks come to each of our grocery store two or three times a week, bringing in food to fill our demands. Of that food, 25%, including all that we grow here, ends up as waste. It's as if every time you go to the grocery story, you leave one whole bag in the parking lot.

"It's not only packaging that is harming Earth's systems, it's rotten food—leftovers not eaten, science projects in the back of the fridge. Also, ugly or unwanted food is the most wasted, we want an 'ugly food table' at our Farmers Markets. Our habits of wasting food will take some conscious work—we need your help to change together."

Jules clicked through beautiful photos, her favorites: one from Cloud 11 Mountain Farm in Boundary, way out to Mountain Cloud Farm in Clark Fork and the flower circle from Greentree Naturals. "We love our farmers: Julie, Breigh, and Diane. Thanks for being here, give us a wave. Of all these Solutions," she clicked back to the list, "the one I am most-most excited about is biochar. I hope you wonder what I am talking about because this was new to me too, but I'm a kid, right? This one really turns me on because it's ancient.

"There's another reason why. Remember the smoke that hung in the valleys locked in by a weather pressure inversion? Those slash piles burned all through November. If all that raw material had been slow-burned in a kiln and oxygen-deprived, there would be no smoke and the result—biochar—would feed our soils for 1,000 years. With anyone who wants to help, we're starting a biochar business! We will bring a kiln to those piles and begin producing a hard, crystal-like form of carbon baked without oxygen." Jules clicked on that slide.

"This is biochar. If you call us with a nice, big pile of nature's waste, we will bring the kiln to your place and leave half the biochar behind for you to re-animate tired soils, which will in turn help mop up vast amounts of CO_2 from the atmosphere. If you're a farmer, you can spread this beautiful carbon on your fields to drawdown more carbon. Nori will come, measure the CO_2 you have captured, and pay you dollars for it."

Silence in the theater. Then Diane stood and began clapping. Pretty soon everyone was on their feet. Jules blushed beet red and bowed slightly. As she sat back down in her wheelchair to rest, she said over the applause, "The best is yet to come."

Sara stepped into that beautiful applause and hugged Jules. "Brilliant." Allowing a little space for her next pronouncement, Sara confessed, "For a couple of months, I thought I had chosen two Sectors that were not very sexy: Cities and Materials. Those are covered in my academic paper, available for you to read at the Reader online."

Her first slide showing *The Work* with her list of solutions, cut right to the chase. "Most of you have a bit of experience with these Solutions. All of them are actual Solutions to reverse global warming, if used efficiently and at scale. One of the secrets to this climate chaos will be doing this work at maximum efficiency. That has rarely, if ever been done. Most Solutions hover around 1 or

146

2 on a scale of 10. Together, we need to reach for the big 10!"

Then she clicked on a slide of Guatemalans walking through Mexico. "These are climate refugees. We've been hearing about them in all kinds of disparaging ways, right? They are not invading the U.S. They come here as their only hope, even though our country has not been hospitable to them."

The next slide was a beautiful collage created by graphic designer Laura Wahl depicting many of the services needed by refugees. "From Maslow's hierarchy of basic psychology, people need food, shelter, clothing, household goods. Whether they come from Guatemala or California, they are going to come here, to our bioregion. I think people are naturally inclined to help those in need. This is where I am going to focus my attention, coming right through the soup kitchens here. If you have been to any one of those daily suppers, you know the number of folks in need doubled in 2019. We have been discovered by climate refugees." She clicked on the iconic picture of Lake Pend Oreille from the top of the Schweitzer chairlift. "Of course, we live in the most beautiful place on Earth.

"One day I looked closely at this word, *Materials*. Taking liberty to stretch recycling a little, I found fast fashion to be the most alarming part of recycling—basically, it is not yet recycled. Most of our fabrics today are made with plastic. Every single time these garments are washed," twirling and holding out her skirts, "tiny pieces of plastic go into the water system. Our sewer recycling process was not designed to take those bits of plastic out of the water. What is that stream of consequence? Half of the water is cleaned enough to be delivered back as drinking water and half goes right on down 130 miles of the Pend Oreille River as food for fish. In this cascading process, it becomes water and food for us. Fast fashion." Sara paused to catch her breath and make eye contact with the audience.

"Raise your hand if you purchased clothing for Christmas." Sara's hand shot in the air. "This outfit is my newest and my last. I am starting a business recycling clothing, redesigning from real fabrics—cotton, hemp, wool, and flax. As I collect and collate other fabrics, those made from petroleum, I will give them to another STEM Project—boys who are starting a business, melting down the plastics from our recycling stream to manufacture outdoor decks and furniture. Brilliant!" Starting and ending with the same word, Sara bowed, smiling broadly, and handed the mic to Alex.

Alex gave time for the audience to buzz and applaud. The Scholars were clapping wildly and hooting. "Right. According to the original Drawdown Scholars, Women and Girls, when combined, equal the # 1 Solution to global warming." She beamed when the audience erupted in spontaneous cheers and clapping.

"It's pretty obvious that the school system is educating our girls well, actually the village—teens in the tipi and the elders who joined us. That's been a different education, a beautiful synergy like the best of Mother Nature. We have talked, grieved, drummed, done lots of ceremony and ritual for gratitude and harmony. Boys and girls together." She didn't rush, but gently clicked through a few of SuZ's best photos of their time in the tipi. "Some of the most powerful work was art therapy and grief work on *#FridaysforFuture*. Thank you, Laura, Maria and Masai. We have many people to thank. Please look at our list of supporters and mentors in your program. We are here because of them."

She had another big surprise for the audience. "Money! I want to start a bank for Women Smallholders. Women who work five acres or less produce half the world's food. To quote the Drawdown book and the website, women smallholders are unpaid or low-paid laborers—they cultivate field and tree crops, tend livestock, and grow home gardens. Most of them are part of the 475 million smallholder families who operate on less than five acres of land.

"I know in our audience—in our counties—many women labor quietly. We want to find all those women, they need our help! When I stretch the definition of smallholders beyond farming, a whole world of entrepreneurial enterprises shows up. I have already asked the eight mayors to revise the cottage industry definition so these women can sell the food they preserve. Most of us were raised on preserved food, but in the winter, when those supplies run out, we go buy canned tomatoes. Right? Why?

"My dad and I are deeply related to the logging business; he quit since I started this project. Dozens of men have drunk gallons of coffee at our kitchen table, first accusing him of abandonment, or worse. The glimmer of hope came when two asked Dad to help them grieve: The past couple of years, loggers have been hell bent on getting the cut-out. That's a logging term for clearcutting every place possible."

Alex clicked on five slides that made people in the audience groan. The first was a clear-cut ridge on the St. Joe. "This beautiful St. Joe River used to be blue-ribbon trout fishing. These two ridges are right across and above the St. Joe. Can you imagine spring runoff right now? And this," pausing for effect, "is the Priest Lake watershed where endangered caribou fight for their last breaths."

She zoomed out to the photos from forest service drones. "These pictures

148

were produced for the forest service to identify more harvestable timber." She flipped to her last two slides. "My Work: I am going to train women to plant trees and Dad will retrain any loggers who want to stop. We have hundreds of acres of tree farms here in this bioregion, but do we know how to regenerate a forest? This is as deeply shaming as anything being done elsewhere on the planet. This is in our backyards, hidden from our view-shed along the Highway 95 corridor. We can't reverse this, but women and girls are going to work with the Native Plant Society—into the woods by the dozens—we will begin to reverse this enormous damage. First, the loggers need to step up and quit responding to the demands for Idaho timber. Most of that demand comes from China. Maybe America is the neediest for toilet paper, in our research we've found that America uses 27,000 trees worth of toilet paper, every day!" She whispered confidently into the mic, "Switch to bamboo, you can't tell the difference but the Earth can."

One person halfway back in the audience yelled, "Sign me up," and the energy of the crowd became electric. "Thank you! Me too. I want to help." Alex pulled her red handkerchief out of her overalls and wiped away her tears. With a little bow, she handed the mic to Dot.

Like her teammates, Dot was well-prepared. "The single most powerful word in this decade will be Regeneration. Regenerating our tired soils and regenerating those clear-cut forests. Regenerating our families and our communities, what does that mean? Before 2030 we will all know the power of this word. It begins with a biology term we learned in 5th grade—photosynthesis—when we followed the sun's ray into a leaf. Remember doing that? Cells multiplied to serve the plant, make its sugar, and those sugars went into the soil as carbon to feed the roots."

Dot was beaming. "This is so simple we take it for granted. This process of regeneration will not only save the planet by storing more and more carbon, we will use this process to regenerate our culture and our businesses, our politics, even our democracy through Earth consciousness. We will all discover unity that's always been there and raise our children to know they are related to all earthly beings. Business-as-usual must regenerate into planet-friendly business enterprises. Like copycats to plants, a process called biomimicry, the fleet of police cars will be electric and so will buses, trucks—every vehicle on the road. All recharged by the Sun.

"My Work: It sounds so simple. I want to document every farm here in our bioregion. It will take quite a lot to interview every farmer and rancher, but Diane has called a regular meeting of farmers and ranchers and I will be there learning what I can. Nori has a process to measure soil carbon, and they will pay farmers for any carbon increases if the farmers sign on to maintain practices that continue to pull more carbon into their soil. For more than 2 million acres, I think this will take a while. Colleen of Solstice Farms said if I wanted to farm and learn how carbon interacts with different crops, I could put her farm back into production. I am no farmer, but she practically insisted I come look when the snow melts. Our mentor Gail says, Solstice Farm is a magical place."

The mic passed to Jules who was their strong finisher. "We found our work in four months or less. Each one of us feels surprised how our passions for one little thread from the 100 Solutions began to form a strong weave. Our learning curves were impossibly steep at times, but we want to leave you with one thing—find what is yours to give. We only ask you to shine. Work is supposed to be as compelling as play. Our elders say, "If not now, then when? If not us, then who? Game on!"

J'nell and Pat came from behind the stage curtain and wrapped the girls in a hug. Now that they had given their presentations, their gifts, they were giggly girls again for a moment. J'nell was quick. "We all have questions. Let them rise naturally. Allow all this glorious Work to sink in. That's what I call composting."

Pat took the mic. "Your questions are welcome. We're going to help the girls answer questions and harvest *The Work* next Friday in the atrium at the Charter School. We described the details on the back page of your program. We all have gifts. You're invited to bring your gifts and tell us what work is play for you. These girls have their junior class finals this coming week. Wish them luck. Be careful out there."

As people filed out, the Consultants gathered up on stage. "Where's Gail? I swear I saw her sitting with us on the front row."

"She never misses a thing," Jules said confidently. "She will be there next week."

EPILOG

Like every circle, cycle or system, the end imagines a new beginning and the spiral ascends. This creature stone felt trapped up the St. Joe River and begged to be relocated. Those clear-cut forests in the Pacific Northwest are a sickness. Mother Earth wants to heal, to perpetuate, to photosynthesize and then to rest after this regeneration, in her cycles. She needs our help now.

Gail was the first one there: This is the way of the Host. After working behind the scenes for five months, she knew it was time to come out of hiding. She was ready to harvest what the girls had produced. Through the week every whiteboard in town was delivered to the Charter School. The Scholars were bringing their Drawdown books to share with the audience. The Harvest agenda had listed only "Ceremony & Gifts." That was all.

Stepping into the school's atrium, Gail gasped with joy at what she saw and tears formed on her lids; she forced them back. On each one of the whiteboards, the Consultants had attached a poster of the book's cover, Laura's artwork, a Tree of Life. The book cover had been enlarged and printed as a bright, big tree. The effect was like stepping into a circular grove of trees. Light streamed in through the atrium windows and made the space feel angelic. Gail did a little sashay around, but soon needed to sit and stop the room from spinning. "Ahhh," she said loudly, like letting the air out of a balloon.

Drawing from her training with Pachamama Alliance, Gail knew what to do first. With heart and gratitude, she borrowed freely from her mentors. Like leaning heavily on a cane, she'd leaned on Mary Alice Arthur, story practitioner and global missionary for Storytelling. It felt radical to follow her advice about story for this Story Harvest. Mary Alice claims that story is subversive, and we can tell a new story simply by choice. Here in this grove of trees was the proof of that.

Janis was there with both hands clapping. She had helped get the Story this far along and sat back to watch the show. The little handout card that Laura Wahl had designed was now enlarged and transformed into this forest. The girls are going to love this, Gail thought.

Her secret preoccupation on the other side of the wrinkle was this creation. The book's debut and signing party would be Memorial Day at The Winery. Why not cause a stir, she said to J'nell in her magnificent barn after the Panida. She had decided to gift the book to anyone who lived in the bioregion. Boxes of books, printed on 100% recycled paper, had already been delivered. Anyone who came to the party would walk away with one. After the Panida event, some people had searched her name and found the new book on Amazon.

So many spirits danced around the ceiling. She could hear Diana say, "Remember, honey, love is all there is! You've never needed anything else for your fuel."

Take the energy in: Everyone brings a gift locked inside of them. Coax it out. People who show up to *The Work* will be game changers.

J'nell and Pat were the next ones to arrive. They would greet the guests, gather names and emails and pass out the Solutions handout. Pat was a foot taller, so she leaned way over to give Gail a hug. "You have stirred up a nest of ants," Pat said. Everyone is scurrying around talking and looking busy."

J'nell looked directly at Gail. "Do you know how many people have watched *Introduction to Drawdown* in this past week?"

Gail said, "I asked my guy at the Library to run it twice a day, every day. How many?"

"I don't know the exact number, probably, hundreds. I watched it twice at home. Thanks for letting us into the Global Commons. Those worldwide groups are quite impressive. Let's start a community here."

Gail's open palms shot straight in the air and she did a yogi back bend. "Glory, hallelujah! That's my dream, my only wish, honey. Let's talk about it today."

Soon the room was abuzz with people who thought they were early. Conversations started with friends first and usually someone saw someone they hadn't seen in ages. It was a great way to begin, everyone talking at once. Gail had borrowed Maria's yoga gong and stood poised to begin on time. The Scholars had come dressed down and very casual.

When Gail rang for the start, the four teens quit hugging people and immediately lined up behind her. All the chairs were set up in two large circles with space between every 4th chair. "Welcome. Welcome. Today we have gathered to reveal our gifts to one another. This is a process, of course. Before we begin, please stand sideways so you have space for an arm reach. We're going to do a somatic exercise that I learned from Staci Hines through Pachamama.

"Somatic spirituality tunes into the vast interior world of wakefulness and joy in our bodies that lies just beneath the surface. Today, we are going to use our bodies to demonstrate spiritual somatics to our minds. Why? Because we want to build an internal bridge between knowing something and being able to act on it. Our bodies hold the sum total of our histories and our conditioning, 3 billion years of evolutionary wisdom. These eons created values like interdependence, empathy, and cooperation. Let's play together.

"To center intentionally, bring your feet about hip-width apart. Be present with your body and with others'. Drop into this place we call center, about an inch below your belly button, energy emanates from this place.

"Bring your breath, your attention, your presence to this soft-belly place ... let yourself drop in. Imagine a 360° bowl here. If you sense any resistance, like muscles holding, let them surrender a bit more to gravity. Feel your connection to the Earth. Simultaneously extend upwards naturally. You can imagine there's a string at the top of your head drawing your body upwards towards the sky. Allow space to form between your vertebrae, let your chin come level. Breathe softly as you feel this length. In somatics, length is the dimension through which we express our dignity. It is also the place we witness dignity in each other.

"While holding onto this length and our dignity, we also want to center in the dimension of our width. Allow yourself to feel your body, side to side. What's my natural width? Relax into that width that allows a feeling of openness. Stretch your arms out. See if you can breathe and feel into that width. Then feel the people around you. Just feel for them. This is a dimension where a lot of us express our boundaries. We can also connect and be vulnerable here.

"Now let's center into the dimension of depth. Hold onto your length, your width, and feel your depth in the back of your body. Feel the back of your head, neck, and the clothes on your body. Feel your butt, the fabric on the back of your legs. Feel your heels. Can you bring more weight to your heels?

"Here we might bring in our Ancestors. Who has your back? Rest into that support. You come from somewhere. Then, move in through your body, feel and soften along your front. If you have glasses on your face, feel those for the tip of your nose. Feel the clothes on your chest and your torso, down your legs. Face into now. Here you are, bring yourself present.

"The last dimension we want to center around is, what do I care about? What is it that I'm here to do? Let whatever that is organize you a bit more. See your truth, feel your length, your dignity. Know that is true and feel your width, your connections. If those are true, how do you relate to your lineage or history? Let it shift something in you. Let it show up in your actions."

Gail paused knowing that for two decades such ceremonies had been her gift to community. "Take a mental moment: What's my mood after this process? What's there? What's showing up? Just let it be with you. Thank you for helping me open our sacred space." Gail paused long enough a familiar restlessness appeared again.

"I have asked for a harvesting of the gifts we all received from these young Scholars. So, if you four will take out your notebooks to support your practice of deep listening, Maria and Masai are going to tell you the story of the past week. Everyone, turn your chairs to face the boards, two long curved rows."

Tina had thought this through the night before. She held a drawing of chairs in a semi-circle with the word boards in the facing circle. "Like this," she beamed. A picture is worth a thousand words. If anyone knew this, it was Tina.

Gail gestured to everyone with her arm circled over her head, turned her chair around, and sat down gently.

Six of the Consultants unstuck the posters and rolled them up for door prizes. The whiteboards had been labeled by Sectors and were now arranged in an arc. At the top of each board, the Sector was written large and below that: "It's all about your gifts, what is yours to do?" Someone had elegant handwriting. Gail was dazzled by all the prep-work that had been done the night before.

"Last week, before a packed crowd at the Panida Theater ..." The story began. Masai went first because she had a thing for leadership and Maria's gift was energy, listening to what was not said. The space between words was really important. "Maria and I kind of camped out in various locations to eavesdrop on the new buzz around town. People heard different things at your presentation and will adopt the Sectors in their own way."

Carefully unsticking her pile of notes, she began with the easy ones. "Women are talking about cooperatives for canning, including a warehouse to hold all they put by this fall." Beautiful round sticky notes began to populate the white boards as Masai harvested the Scholars' work and dished it back to them. Walk More. Green Buildings. Plant Yards. Land Sharing. Cobb Houses. Tree Farms. Four Seasons. Four Generations.

Maria chimed in, "At the library and the Co-op, I heard the excitement. Even at the lunch tables at the Samuels Store the server told me they've heard the buzzing. Congratulations! *The Work* has just begun—well, you know this. What you don't know is how your ideas will evolve in the creative hearts of people who are waking up."

Maria pulled more sticky notes out of her pocket. "These are from the kids in the tipi this afternoon. Everyone is glad finals are over. The graduating seniors are a little dazed. Some have refined their college plans to include Earth sciences." She added Tree Planting Expeditions and elders' Front Yards.

On each one of the white boards, Maria stuck a note that said Jobs. Six notes read Jobs written large. "This may be your biggest contribution." Then she went one Sector at a time. Under Food she stuck Food Systems, Home Canning Warehouse and Diane's Farmstand Model. Below the words Land Use the sticky notes read Shared Farming, Re-wilding, NPS for Native Plant Society.

"This last one came from a couple of 14-year-old twins who plan to learn the flora of our bioregion and help plant the understory where trees are being planted. They said they met Marilyn and JD up Grouse Creek last year."

Masai took another turn, she had more sticky notes and made a quick round of the whiteboards. She also had another idea. "It's time to engage you, all of you. J'nell and Pat provided these blank sticky notes and markers. What is yours to do? Stand up and take the floor for two or three minutes and tell us how these Drawdown Scholars touched you. Did they ignite anything resting in your hearts?"

Three people stood and decided who went first and second. "I'm a tree planter. I love that young kids want to go on expeditions into the woods to restore our damaged forests. Since I've worked 30 years for Idaho Lands, I want to serve our local woods and I need to get off my butt. This is how I want to spend my pension, restoring forests."

"For me, I have an empty building on the edge of town. I want to donate it to the canning queens. It does need insulation and heating, but my husband needs a project this summer."

A third woman stood and said, "I haven't forgotten that in another life I was a seamstress. I want to work with Sara and the Community Action League (CAL) and all those beautiful women of Bizarre Bazaar to gather discards from everyone's closet and produce all new clothing made from perfectly good, natural fibers. We do need to eliminate the plastic fibers."

Three seniors stood next and Samantha spoke for the group, "We're about to graduate and for that we feel gratitude to many of you in this room. Sure, we did the schoolwork, but you raised us. We adore the saying, 'It takes a village,' because we feel it. This summer we are going to work with Alex to take kids – age appropriate of course – into the woods to mark our precious trees by GPS. In between finals, I contacted three of our local tree farms. They are going to donate good starts, as much as 10 % of their inventory, little trees now five years old that we can bundle and carry up the watershed to restore our forests." She walked over to the woman who had talked first. "With your 30 years of experience, will you be our leader? We're just kids, after all."

The meeting went on for two more hours, until the room began to feel drained of its energy. Everyone dug into the pizzas that were delivered when the discussion ended. Gail closed her eyes to enjoy the buzz of everyone talking at once. She thought of her teachers and offered silent gratitude for this harvest.

Hattie sat down in the chair next to Gail and said, "I knew you had this in you. The Scholars touched me so deeply last week. I cried all the way through their presentations. Two of them came through my kindergarten, you know."

Just two weeks earlier, Gail attended Hattie's closing party for three- and four-year-old children. It was Hattie who graduated this year. Like all her Mayfairs of the past two decades, the children were dressed in their finest, the spring flowers they held for the parade, forsythia and apple blossoms, were abundant. Like every year, everyone enjoyed the Maypole dance.

After the mothers had given speeches, Gail had said to the crowd, "This has been the single-most heart-felt gift I have ever witnessed. For nearly 30 years Hattie has been singing children through their day, into the woods, and on their way home with happy parents. Thank you for allowing me to be your witness, Hattie."

"That's it, right? You're retiring too?"

"I think *The Work* has just begun. As I switch off the Waldorf kindergarten, I am going to switch on restoring wild bees. You and I get to enjoy the show from our camp chairs. This community we dreamed about is finally forming." Gail lifted up Hattie's hand and planted a kiss.

The very next day, Gail registered the *Kootenai Region Pachamama Community* in the Global Commons of the Pachamama Alliance.

The end signals a new beginning and the spiral ascends. oxoxo

A LITTLE PRAYER

From Coyote to Earth, a remembering prayer: Sweet Mother,
Through your coddling and nourishment, you have become alive inside me,
I feel you.

Evacuating, I see you, it all began with dirty diapers a few decades back
Gradually awakening to find you inside of me, turning my life to you,
I became We.

Forgetfulness lasts way too long. Many have even forgotten our own star.
Until we all remember, can we make plans to help you, dear Mother Earth?
You and your trees have always known what to do,
We ask you to evolve our thoughts
If you will guide our wakefulness, we will learn agroforestry and silvoculture.

With your guidance, dear Earth, we will become shapeshifters to bi-locate,
Our seeds will quicken, we will discover the wonder of dropping into a forest
Many choose a quivering forest of Quaking Aspens, they exquisitely reveal
Interconnected beings, interbeing, a forest of truths we honor by visiting.

Experiencing such wild places, we fall in love with protection as life itself
Shapeshift into Coyote and tell stories to make us laugh from our bellies.
Did you hear the one about the old Mentor who knew she could bi-locate?

One story follows another.
Coyote teaches us how to move through a wrinkle in time.

LAST WORD

Coyote takes a look.
This time, at a 3-year-old boy, it's just a look.
Boy looks back. Being seen is everything.

We are meant to co-inhabit, co-exist, to find harmony,
and to see each other.
Can we rise to this challenge?

Books Honorably Mentioned

Dolores LaChapelle, *Deep Powder Snow: 40 Years of Ecstatic Skiing, Avalanches, and Earth Wisdom (1993)*.

Rachel Carson, *Silent Spring (1962)*.

Ruth H. Howes and Caroline C. Herzenberg, *Their Day in the Sun: Women of the Manhattan Project (1999)*.

Paul Hawken, Editor, *Drawdown: The Most Comprehensive Plan Ever Proposed to Reverse Global Warming (2016)*.

Madeleine L'Engle, *A Wrinkle in Time (1962)*.

Richard Powers, *The Overstory: A Novel (2018)*.

Albert Bates and Kathleen Draper, *Burn: Using Fire to Save the Planet (2019)*.

Other Notable Mentions
Nori.com (for carbon credits)
Drawdown.org (for inspiration), here comes Drawdown 2.0
Pachamama Alliance.org (for The Work)
Connect.globalcommons.org for the Drawdown movie
Ninepassages.com (for connection and community)

Inspirations Not Mentioned
Christiana Figueres and Tom Rivett-Carnac *The Future We Choose: Surviving the Climate Crisis* (2020).

Christopher Ketcham *This Land: How Cowboys, Capitalism and Corruption are Ruining the American West. (2019)*.

Robin Wall Kimmerer *Braiding Sweetgrass: Indigenous Wisdom, Scientific Knowledge and The Teachings of Plants* (2013). Also, *Gathering Moss (2003)*.

Kristin Ohlson *The Soil Will Save Us: How Scientists, Farmers, and Ranchers Are Tending the Soil to Reverse Global Warming.*

David W. Orr *Dangerous Years: Climate Change, the Long Emergency, and the Way Forward* (2017).

David Wallace-Wells *The Uninhabitable Earth: Life After Warming* (2019).

Margaret W. Wheatley *Who Do We Choose to Be?* And all others, especially *Warriors for the Human Spirit: A Songline* (2020).

Rebecca Solnit *A Paradise Built in Hell* (2010). And all other works.

Find these growing lists at www.ninepassages.com
Characters in the book
Beloved Teachers
Books
Poetry
Blog Posts on Passages
Stories of Wildlife Refuges

Curating other inspirations, have a look: sign up to stay connected.
Ninepassages.com — Story Activist::Writer and Elder Mentor
Facebook.com/authorgailburkett/

Ninepassages.com-- Story Activist::Writer and Elder Mentor
Facebook.com/authorgailburkett/

Printed in Great Britain
by Amazon

85446183R00093